SUCCEED AT
PSYCHOMETRIC TESTING

PRACTICE TESTS FOR
THE ARMED FORCES
ENTRY LEVEL

BERNICE WALMSLEY

SUCCEED AT
PSYCHOMETRIC TESTING

PRACTICE TESTS FOR
THE ARMED FORCES
ENTRY LEVEL

Hodder Arnold

A MEMBER OF THE HODDER HEADLINE GROUP

For order enquiries please contact Bookpoint Ltd, 130 Milton Park, Abingdon, Oxon OX14 4SB. Telephone: (44) 01235 827720. Fax: (44) 01235 400454. Lines are open from 9.00–18.00, Monday to Saturday, with a 24-hour message answering service. Details about our titles and how to order are available at www.hoddereducation.com

British Library Cataloguing in Publication Data
A catalogue record for this title is available from the British Library

ISBN-10: 0340 926554
ISBN-13: 978 0340 926 550

First published   2006
Impression number 10 9 8 7 6 5 4 3 2 1
Year   2010   2009   2008   2007   2006

The publisher has used its best endeavours to ensure that the URLs for external websites referred to in this book are correct and active at the time of going to press. However, the publisher and the author have no responsibility for the websites and can make no guarantee that a site will remain live or that the content will remain relevant, decent, or appropriate.

Typeset by Servis Filmsetting Ltd, Longsight, Manchester.
Printed in Great Britain for Hodder Education,
a division of Hodder Headline, 338 Euston Road, London NW1 3BH
by Cox & Wyman Ltd, Reading, Berkshire.

Hodder Headline's policy is to use papers that are natural, renewable and recyclable products and made from wood grown in sustainable forests. The logging and manufacturing processes are expected to conform to the environmental regulations of the country of origin.

Contents

Foreword

If anyone tells you that it is impossible to improve your score in a psychometric test, don't pay any attention. It isn't true.

A multi-million pound industry has developed around the notion that psychometric tests yield accurate and true data about an individual's ability. While this is generally the case, test results can differ widely and are determined by a range of factors, including the test environment, the professionalism and experience of the test administrator, the level of confidence of the candidate on the day of the test, the candidate's familiarity with the testing process, and the amount of practice a candidate has had prior to the test.

As the industry develops, test-takers are becoming more informed about what is expected of them, and about what they should expect from the testing process. Increasingly, candidates are taking control of the process, and demonstrating that it is feasible to prepare for psychometric tests and to significantly improve scores.

This series of books was designed with you, the test-taker, in mind. In finding this book you have demonstrated a commitment to achieving your potential in the upcoming test.

Commitment and confidence play a large role in determining your level of success, and practice will help to build your confidence.

A common complaint from candidates is that they cannot find enough material to practise. This series aims to overcome this deficiency by providing you with chapter after chapter of timed tests for you to take under test conditions. The series covers many examples of question sets appropriate to the major test publishers, and will help you to prepare for numerical, verbal, logical, abstract and diagrammatic reasoning tests.

Chapter 1 offers you specific advice on how to prepare for your test. Once you have read through the instructions in Chapter 1, go straight to the timed tests in Chapter 2. Be sure to set aside enough time to finish a complete test at one sitting – the timings are given at the beginning of each test. Chapter 3 lists all the answers to the questions in Chapter 2 in one place, so that you can quickly check off the answers, and Chapter 4 provides you with the explanations. If you have time, wait a few days before retaking the tests – at least enough time to have forgotten the answers. In between taking and retaking the tests in this series, practise with other sources. You will find a list of these in Chapter 5.

Few people enjoy psychometric tests. Yet if psychometric tests are the major obstacle between you and your perfect job, it is worth spending some time learning how to get beyond this obstacle. You can be proactive in achieving your best score by practising as much as you can.

Finally, if you don't achieve your best score at your first attempt, try again. You may be pleasantly surprised by your results the second time around. Good luck!

Heidi Smith
Series Editor

The other titles in the series are:
Numerical Reasoning Intermediate
Numerical Reasoning Advanced
Verbal Reasoning Intermediate
Verbal Reasoning Advanced
Diagrammatic and Abstract Reasoning
Data Interpretation
The National Police Selection Process
Critical Verbal Reasoning

CHAPTER 1

Introduction

WHO SHOULD READ THIS BOOK?

This book is aimed at anyone who is considering applying for entry to the Armed Forces of the United Kingdom to learn a trade. This, then, includes entry as a soldier in the Army, a rating in the Navy and an aircraftman/woman in the Air Force. To enter the Armed Forces you will have to successfully negotiate the appropriate selection process, according to which service you have chosen. The selection procedures for all three services include tests to discover your abilities in a variety of areas and reflect the specific demands of the jobs available in the Army, the Air Force or the Navy. Written tests and exercises of this nature are often a stumbling block and can make even the best candidate worried, but they are certainly something that you can prepare for and improve your performance. This is the purpose of this book.

As you would expect, the tests and exercises for entry at Officer level are more extensive and, as such, are outside the scope of this book.

Testing yourself on actual examples of the types of questions and tests that you will encounter is vital. Then, and only then, can you assess where your efforts to improve need to be concentrated. Be reassured, it is perfectly possible to improve your score.

In this book there will be a little theory about each of the types of tests and then plenty of practice. Not only will you improve the scores you can achieve in the selection process for the service of your choice but the familiarity that comes from the extended practice available in this book will also raise your confidence level overall. This extra confidence will help to improve your general performance at interview. You will find lots of examples for you to work through and some handy tips on how to tackle them. We will be examining the common pitfalls associated with these tests and then discovering how to avoid them.

WHAT ARE THE RECRUITERS LOOKING FOR?

Each of the three Armed Forces is looking for the very best recruits to suit their requirements – and the requirements of each of the services and of the individual jobs for which they are recruiting will vary. Each service will insist on your being physically fit and will have their own criteria and tests for this.

The aptitude tests that you will have to sit, no matter which of the services you are aiming for, are the focus of this book but there will also be interviews and physical tests and your existing academic qualifications (if any) will also be taken into account. It will therefore be useful at this stage to look briefly at each of the services in turn to see what they will be looking for.

The Army

To qualify for entry into the Army, applicants must be residents of the United Kingdom, Irish Republic or be a Commonwealth citizen and should normally be between 16 and 29 years old on the day of enlistment (check with your local recruiting office for possible exceptions to this). If you are under 18 you will need parental consent.

The tests that you will take for entrance to the Army assess your suitability for training and your results will determine what sort of training you are offered. Only a few types of training require specific qualifications, certain technical jobs for example. There will also be a fitness test.

For more information on Army recruitment, go to www. armyjobs.co.uk.

The Navy

The selection process for ratings for the Navy takes place at a local Armed Forces Careers Office and consists of the Navy's aptitude tests. At a later date there is a Careers Advice interview and a medical examination followed by a security questionnaire.

For further information on Navy recruitment, visit www.royal-navy.mod.uk.

The Air Force

The Air Force will, in addition to the aptitude tests that will be described in detail later in this chapter, also conduct a number of interviews (a selection interview, a specialist interview where appropriate, and a final interview) and a medical. The interviews aim to identify people who are suitable for training. You will have to pass each stage of the selection process before you move on to the next.

For more information on recruitment to the Air Force, see www. rafcareers.com.

HOW AND WHEN WILL YOU SIT THE TESTS?

The recruitment processes for each of the Armed Forces have a number of stages that you have to get through in order to be accepted into the service of your choice. It is therefore vital that you give your very best performance during this process.

The Armed Forces, in common with most other large employers, use standardised tests as a technique to help them select the best candidates. These are the ones that will be capable of meeting the demands of the job. Of course, there is a vast range of jobs and trades on offer in each of the services so the tests at this level assess generally required skills and aptitudes such as your ability to use numbers or English and your understanding of basic mechanical principles.

First, of course, you will have to complete an application form that will ask for a lot of information about you. This will ensure that you meet the requirements such as age, nationality, health, physique, eyesight and education that each service will require. If you meet these requirements then you will be invited to an Armed Forces Careers Office to sit the aptitude tests and have an interview. To be successful at this stage you will also need to prove your physical and medical fitness.

The aim of the aptitude tests is to assess your potential future performance. The selection process for a career in the UK Armed Forces is a lengthy one and will be followed by a probationary period in the service.

WHAT SORTS OF TEST WILL YOU BE GIVEN?

As the requirements of each of the Armed Forces are slightly different, there are different sets of tests that you will have to negotiate according to the service you have chosen. Let's look at each of the services:

The Army

The tests (collectively referred to as 'BARB' – the British Army Recruit Battery) you are given during the recruitment procedures for the Army all use a computer touch screen and are not timed. It takes, on average, about **30 minutes** to complete all **five tests** and the number of questions that are shown to you in each part varies according to the speed at which you work. The test is set up in such a way that there is no 'pass or fail'. The higher your score, the greater choice of trades will be offered to you. The battery of tests comprises:

1 Reasoning: Here you are given a sentence about two people and you must answer the questions given to you. It is a problem-solving test.

2 Letter Checking: In this test your ability to carry out a checking process is assessed.

3 Number Distance: This tests your ability to use numbers quickly and accurately by calculating the differences between three numbers.

4 Odd One Out: Here you have to select the odd one out from a group of three words, so it checks your understanding of the English language.

5 Symbol Rotation: This tests your spatial awareness by identifying which shapes are the same when rotated.

The Navy

Here again you have a battery of tests to get through. They are as follows:

1 Reasoning: This is a test of your verbal reasoning skills and involves spotting connections between words and their meanings. This part of the test has **30 questions** and lasts **9 minutes**.

2 English Language: Your ability to use the English language correctly will be tested here with a part again comprising **30 questions** to be answered in **9 minutes**.

3 Numeracy: This part which again consists of **30 questions** but with a longer time allowed – **16 minutes** – tests your ability to use numbers.

4 Mechanical Comprehension: Here your understanding of basic mechanical concepts will be tested. There are **30 questions** for which you are allowed **10 minutes**.

The Air Force

The battery of tests you will have to sit for entry into the Air Force is wide-ranging and tests your abilities in a variety of areas:

1 Verbal Reasoning: In this test you are presented with information then asked questions that check your ability to understand and use written information. It consists of **20 questions** to be answered in **15 minutes**.

2 Numerical Reasoning: This test is in two parts. The first consists of questions that involve fractions, decimals and formulae and has **12 questions** for which you are allowed **4 minutes**. In the second part your ability to interpret and use numerical information presented in tables and graphs is tested. This part has **15 questions** to be answered in **11 minutes**.

3 Work Rate: This test comprises coding exercises that are used to test how quickly and accurately you can work. There are **20 questions** to be answered in **4 minutes**.

4 Spatial Reasoning: Again this is a test that comes in two parts. The first part tests your ability to work with shapes and objects and has **10 questions** to be answered in **4 minutes**. The second part uses similar objects and shapes but this time they are three-dimensional and you have to say what they will look like after they have been rotated. You will have **10 questions** to answer in **3 minutes**.

5 Electrical Comprehension: Here you will be asked **21 questions** about basic electrical concepts. You will have **11 minutes** to answer them.

6 Mechanical Comprehension: This tests your ability to work with mechanical concepts and has **20 questions** to be answered in **10 minutes**.

7 Memory: This tests how accurately you can remember information. There are two parts to the test, both of which are presented on film. The first part tests your ability to remember sequences of letters and the second part presents patterns to test your memory. Both parts have **10 questions** each and timing is driven by the length of each film.

WHY ARE TESTS NECESSARY?

The varied nature of the work on offer in each of the Armed Forces means that recruiters must not only be certain that the people they choose will be able to cope well with the job but also that they are particularly suited to the training for the type of work being offered. Some of the attributes that they are looking for can be discovered during interviews or physical ability tests, but others are less obvious and it is these abilities that the selection processes are designed to find.

From an employer's point of view, interviewing and taking on staff is an expensive and risky business and the Armed Forces are no exception to this. There are a number of ways in which aptitude testing can help them:

- Each service receives a large number of applicants and tests can whittle down the number to a more manageable and cost-effective level.

- Tests can be combined with other selection procedures to enable the recruiter to make better decisions.

- Tests are much less subjective than interviews alone – this is better for the recruiter and for the interviewees.

- Better decisions at this stage will result in fewer people leaving the services prematurely.

- Selecting the right recruits will reduce induction costs or wasted training.

- Employing the right people will lead to a reduction in the possibility of potentially dangerous or costly mistakes being made by an incompetent recruit.

- CVs are notoriously unreliable. Anyone can declare that they are numerate or literate or have knowledge of electronics or mechanical concepts – tests will show whether or not this is actually true.

With these reasons in mind, we can see that any employer would be well advised to find a more efficient way of selecting staff than interviews alone. Mistakes in recruitment are expensive. Employers frequently use aptitude tests as an additional tool to help with their decision-making – especially if they have a large number of applicants – and the selection process of each of the three Armed Forces includes a set of tests designed specifically to discover the aptitudes that are desirable – or even essential – in a soldier, a sailor or an aircraftman/woman.

HOW TO USE THIS BOOK

The tests in the main part of this book are timed where appropriate and the answers and explanations – including tips on how to tackle the questions and some pitfalls to avoid related to the specific questions – will be contained in chapters separate from the questions (chapters 3 and 4) so that you will be able to test yourself in a situation as close to the actual test conditions as possible. However, as an introduction to the types of questions and how you can use this book, we will quickly run through the whole question/answer/explanation process. Here are a few examples of the type of question you may encounter when you sit real tests for each of the three services:

The Army

REASONING

Question

Read and memorise the sentence then answer the question relating to it.

Sally is not as slim as Jean.

Who is fatter?

a Sally

b Jean

Answer

a Sally

Explanation

Where a sentence is stated in the negative as it is here, it can make things less confusing if you re-phrase it as a positive statement, i.e. 'Sally is fatter than Jean' or 'Jean is slimmer than Sally'. It is easy then to answer the question.

LETTER CHECKING

Question

Look at the four pairs of letters, shown one above the other. One of each pair will be upper case (a capital letter) and the other will be lower case (a small letter). Decide whether the two letters in each pair are the same and then calculate how many matching pairs there are in each set of four.

b	c	d	e
C	E	D	B

  a 0

  b 1

  c 2

  d 3

  e 4

Answer

  b 1

Explanation

The easy way to go about this sort of test is to check each individual pair of letters and to keep a tally of the matching pairs as you go along.

NUMBER DISTANCE

Question

Each question consists of three numbers. Your task is to find the largest and the smallest numbers and then to decide which of these is further away from the remaining number.

9   13   20

- **a** 9
- **b** 13
- **c** 20

Answer

- **c** 20

Explanation

The highest figure is 20 and is 7 away from the middle figure, while 9 is the smallest number and is only 4 away from the middle number, so 20 is the answer.

ODD ONE OUT

Question

Each question consists of three words. Two of the words will be connected – they may be opposites or have similar meanings. You must indicate the odd one out.

calm   small   little

   a   calm

   b   small

   c   little

Answer

   a   calm

Explanation

Small and little have similar meanings but calm has no connection with these two words so calm is the answer.

The Navy

REASONING

Question

Choose the correct word from the choices given.

Full is to empty as deep is to?:

   a   shallow

   b   flowing

   c   cut

   d   skin

   e   part

Answer

a shallow

Explanation

Empty is the opposite in meaning to full so you must find the opposite of deep – shallow.

ENGLISH LANGUAGE

Question

Which of the following words is the odd one out?

a new
b unused
c outdated
d original
e fresh

Answer

c outdated

Explanation

Four words in this group of five have similar meanings, and in this case these are new, unused, original and fresh, so outdated is the one that does not fit in that group.

NUMERACY

Question

Solve the following problem without using a calculator.

A man walks for 30 minutes. If he walks at six miles an hour, how far will he have travelled?

- **a** 12 miles
- **b** 2 miles
- **c** 0.5 mile
- **d** 6 miles
- **e** 3 miles

Answer

- **e** 3 miles

Explanation

If the man walks for half an hour, then he will only walk half the distance that he would walk in an hour so divide his speed for one hour by two to get your answer.

MECHANICAL COMPREHENSION

Question

Why would a fridge not work efficiently if packed with too much food?

a It will get too cold.

b The air will not be able to circulate.

c You would not be able to see everything.

d It might be the wrong type of food.

e There will be a power failure.

Answer

b The air will not be able to circulate.

Explanation

This requires you to know that convection currents cool food in a fridge so air must be allowed to circulate to allow it to work properly.

The Air Force

VERBAL REASONING

Question

Read the following information then answer the question.

Cinema A is showing a comedy.

Cinema B is showing a historical romance.

Cinema C is showing a science fiction thriller.

Which Cinema would the following family choose to visit?

They have two small children who may be frightened by science fiction, Mum doesn't like thrillers and Dad can't stand romantic films.

Answer

Cinema A

Explanation

You should tackle this sort of question systematically. Science fiction is out because of the children, the mother does not like thrillers, and romantic films are ruled out by the father so the only possible choice is the comedy at Cinema A.

NUMERICAL REASONING

Question

Solve the following without using a calculator.

Calculate 27 divided by 3.

  a 81
  b 1.0
  c 30
  d 9
  e 0.9

Answer

  d 9

Explanation

This should be a straightforward question – you may know the answer straight away – but do not get confused by decimal points or by multiplying instead of dividing (answer **a** 81 is there deliberately to confuse).

ELECTRICAL COMPREHENSION

Question

Which item would use more electricity?

a   a reading lamp

b   a kettle

c   a radio

Answer

b   a kettle

Explanation

Electricity can be used to produce heat, movement and light. Of these heat uses the most electricity.

NOW TRY THE TESTS

Hopefully you are now convinced that preparation, including testing yourself using the tests in this book, will definitely improve your performance – and your chances of getting into the Armed Force of your choice. So, on with the tests . . .

CHAPTER 2

Timed tests

SECTION 1 – THE ARMY

Unlike the other two services, the tests for the Army are not timed and the number of questions given to you in each part is adjusted according to your speed. This is done automatically, as you take the test on a computer monitor. You should work as quickly and accurately as you can.

Army Test 1

REASONING

Read and memorise the sentence then answer the question relating to it. Remember that in the actual test you will not see the question on the screen at the same time as the answers.

1   Pete is taller than Sam.

Who is shorter?

a   Pete

b   Sam

2 Norman arrived earlier than John.

Who arrived later?

a Norman

b John

3 Pam has lighter hair than Sue.

Who has darker hair?

a Pam

b Sue

4 Ali reads fewer books than Andrew.

Who reads more books?

a Ali

b Andrew

5 Carole has more shoes than Barbara.

Who has fewer shoes?

a Carole

b Barbara

6 Fiona is not as short as Ann.

Who is taller?

a Fiona

b Ann

7 Paul is a better cricketer than John.

Who is worse at cricket?

a Paul

b John

8 Brinda is slower than Kate.

Who is faster?

a Brinda

b Kate

9 John is heavier than Bob.

Who is lighter?

a John

b Bob

10 Fran is not as strong as Betty.

Who is stronger?

a Fran

b Betty

11 Colin is not as tall as Angus.

Who is shorter?

a Colin

b Angus

12 Pat is not as strong as Eve.

Who is weaker?

a Pat

b Eve

13 Bill is not as optimistic as Fred.

Who is more optimistic?

a Bill

b Fred

14 Kath is happier than Millie.

Who is less happy?

a Kath

b Millie

15 Nigel lives in a bigger house than Michael.

Who lives in a smaller house?

a Nigel

b Michael

16 Diane is not as good as Janet.

Who is worse?

a Diane

b Janet

17 Ellie is sadder than Olivia.

Who is happier?

a　Ellie

b　Olivia

18 Carl is not as bright as Wilson.

Who is duller?

a　Carl

b　Wilson

19 Bob is not as strong as Sam.

Who is weaker?

a　Bob

b　Sam

20 Zoë is not as dull as Anna.

Who is brighter?

a　Zoë

b　Anna

Answers on page 145.

Army Test 2

LETTER CHECKING

Look at the four pairs of letters. One of each pair will be upper case (a capital letter) and the other will be lower case (a small letter) – one of each pair will be on the top row and the other will be on the row directly below it. Decide whether the two letters in each pair are the same and then calculate how many matching pairs there are in each set of four, making your choice of answer from those (**a–e**) given below each question.

1 a   f   g   x
     A   L   G   X

a 0
b 1
c 2
d 3
e 4

2 G   X   Y   Z
    g   x   y   z

a 0
b 1
c 2
d 3
e 4

3 a   l   m   n
    E   F   N   M

a 0
b 1
c 2
d 3
e 4

4   s   e   b   c
   B   C   A   C

a   0
b   1
c   2
d   3
e   4

5   S   C   R   P
   c   s   r   p

a   0
b   1
c   2
d   3
e   4

6   N   B   S   F
   n   b   s   f

a   0
b   1
c   2
d   3
e   4

7

X	C	L	M
x	c	i	d

a 0

b 1

c 2

d 3

e 4

8

H	W	Q	S
h	w	r	s

a 0

b 1

c 2

d 3

e 4

9

g	s	t	v
G	S	T	V

a 0

b 1

c 2

d 3

e 4

10 B   T   E   S
     d   t   b   s

a 0
b 1
c 2
d 3
e 4

11 F   W   M   L
     b   f   n   w

a 0
b 1
c 2
d 3
e 4

12 D   S   F   U
     o   s   f   u

a 0
b 1
c 2
d 3
e 4

13 T   E   Y   B

     e   t   y   b

a 0
b 1
c 2
d 3
e 4

14 S   F   L   G

     s   l   f   g

a 0
b 1
c 2
d 3
e 4

15 b   d   h   l

     D   E   H   J

a 0
b 1
c 2
d 3
e 4

16   q   l   m   s
      Q   L   M   F

a   0
b   1
c   2
d   3
e   4

17   R   S   T   U
      u   r   s   t

a   0
b   1
c   2
d   3
e   4

18   l   o   p   c
      M   O   P   D

a   0
b   1
c   2
d   3
e   4

19

M	Z	F	X
m	z	e	s

a 0

b 1

c 2

d 3

e 4

20

s	n	f	o
X	S	F	O

a 0

b 1

c 2

d 3

e 4

Answers on Page 146.

Army Test 3

NUMBER DISTANCE

Each question consists of three numbers. Your task is to find the largest and the smallest numbers in the set of three and then to decide which of these is further away from the remaining number.

1   4   3   7

a   4
b   3
c   7

2   9   11   20

a   9
b   11
c   20

3   6   14   3

a   6
b   14
c   3

4   20   17   11

a   20
b   17
c   11

5   19   12   3

a   19
b   12
c   3

6   6   18   10

a   6
b   18
c   10

7   14   2   3

a   14
b   2
c   3

8   7   14   19

a   7
b   14
c   19

9   3   11   12

a   3
b   11
c   12

10 5   3   8

a   5
b   3
c   8

11 18   3   12

a 18
b 3
c 12

12 9   4   19

a 9
b 4
c 19

13 17   6   3

a 17
b 6
c 3

14 17   19   2

a 17
b 19
c 2

15 8   4   19

a 8
b 4
c 19

16 2　　11　　7

a 2

b 11

c 7

17 1　　4　　11

a 1

b 4

c 11

18 8　　15　　3

a 8

b 15

c 3

19 6　　9　　1

a 6

b 9

c 1

20 4　　20　　10

a 4

b 20

c 10

Answers on page 146.

Army Test 4

ODD ONE OUT

Each question consists of three words. Two of the words will be connected – they may be opposites, have similar meanings or be related in some way. You must indicate the odd one out.

1 fat   bus   thin

a fat
b bus
c thin

2 common   rug   carpet

a common
b rug
c carpet

3 sail   also   boat

a sail
b also
c boat

4 bad   good   drastic

a bad
b good
c drastic

5   seven   zoo   animal

a   seven

b   zoo

c   animal

6   dry   meeting   appointment

a   dry

b   meeting

c   appointment

7   sweet   picture   sour

a   sweet

b   picture

c   sour

8   dismantle   assemble   cooperate

a   dismantle

b   assemble

c   cooperate

9   devious   happy   sad

a   devious

b   happy

c   sad

10 dark　　　light　　　evening

a　dark

b　light

c　evening

11 camera　　　pick　　　choose

a　camera

b　pick

c　choose

12 several　　　many　　　chair

a　several

b　many

c　chair

13 meet　　　late　　　early

a　meet

b　late

c　early

14 stand　　　pullover　　　sit

a　stand

b　pullover

c　sit

15 fall   nasty   nice

a fall

b nasty

c nice

16 coins   change   furniture

a coins

b change

c furniture

17 sky   sound   noise

a sky

b sound

c noise

18 careful   sleep   doze

a careful

b sleep

c doze

19 criminal   temper   crook

a criminal

b temper

c crook

20 master   mistress   star

a   master

b   mistress

c   star

Answers on page 147.

Army Test 5

SYMBOL ROTATION

Each question consists of two boxes, both of which contain a pair of shapes. These shapes may have been rotated on the page. You must decide how many of the boxes (0, 1 or 2) contain two shapes – one above the other – that are exactly the same after being rotated.

1

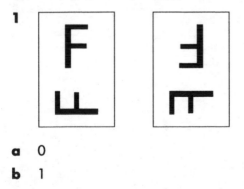

a   0

b   1

c   2

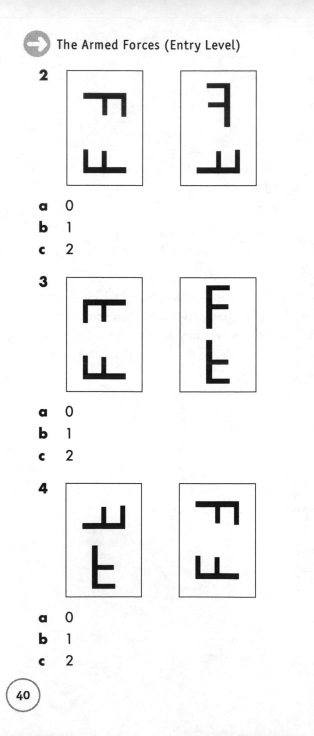

2

a 0
b 1
c 2

3

a 0
b 1
c 2

4

a 0
b 1
c 2

5

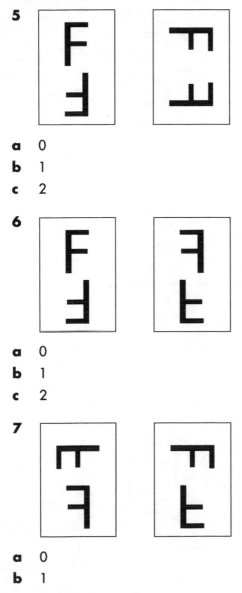

a 0
b 1
c 2

6

a 0
b 1
c 2

7

a 0
b 1
c 2

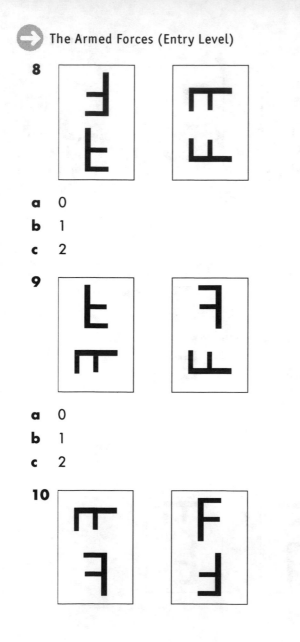

8

a   0
b   1
c   2

9

a   0
b   1
c   2

10

a 0

b 1

c 2

Answers on page 147.

SECTION 2 – THE NAVY

Navy Test 1

REASONING

Choose the correct word from the choices given. You are allowed 9 minutes to complete this test.

1 Minute is to hour as day is to:

a second

b clock

c calendar

d week

e time

2 Hunger is to food as thirst is to:

a starvation

b drink

c thirsty

d beer

e swallow

3 Last is to final as first is to:

a almost

b win

c early

d soon

e initial

4 Sweet is to sugar as bitter is to:

a banana

b lemon

c potato

d bread

e food

5 Chapter is to book as verse is to:

a poem

b rhyme

c writing

d poet

e newspaper

6 Wheel is to car as rudder is to:

a sailor

b ship

c steer

d train

e sail

7 Dark is to night as light is to:

a midnight

b day

c sunshine

d bulb

e noon

8 Pudding is to dessert as soup is to:

a sweet

b savoury

c starter

d main course

e stew

9 Calendar is to date as book is to:

a cover

b index

c bookshop

d time

e word

10 Several is to many as hardly any is to:

a countless

b numerous

c few

d inadequate

e least

11 Widespread is to extensive as limited is to:

a confined

b intensive

c few

d company

e prevalent

12 Ramble is to hike as stroll is to:

a marathon

b slowly

c run

d walk

e climb

13 Oral is to talk as aural is to:

a hear

b speak

c ears

d feel

e smell

14 Coin is to money as book is to:

a volume

b buy

c currency

d library

e read

15 Male is to female as hero is to:

a coward

b adventure

c brave

d man

e courage

16 Perfection is to flaw as triumph is to:

a faultless

b cataclysm

c loss

d win

e gain

17 Wicket is to cricket as goalpost is to:

a football

b game

c score

d goal

e goalkeeper

18 Adjournment is to delay as imperfection is to:

a time

b pure

c perfection

d defect

e perfect

19 Mate is to friend as marry is to:

a wedding

b get hitched

c dress

d engaged

e ring

20 Author is to book as potter is to:

a ceramic

b pot

c clay

d kiln

e throw

21 Word is to dictionary as track is to:

a compact disc

b run

c book

d rail

e definition

22 Stitch is to sewing machine as press is to:

a seam

b steam

c sew

d board

e iron

23 View is to television as listen is to:

a speak

b radio

c programme

d see

e hear

24 Mobile is to move as immobile is to:

a agitate

b active

c still

d first

e wander

25 Stock is to warehouse as livestock is to:

a cattle

b goods

c buy

d farm

e dead

26 Sticky is to glue as greasy is to:

a water

b oil

c fry

d lubricate

e pan

27 Farmer is to field as policeman is to:

a criminal

b crime

c report

d work

e beat

28 Fly is to plane as sail is to:

a sailor

b boat

c train

d row

e cruise

29 Clock is to time as dictionary is to:

a find

b check

c definition

d opposite

e book

30 Motorway is to car as track is to:

a drive

b train

c fast

d race

e locate

Answers on page 148.

Navy Test 2

ENGLISH LANGUAGE

Which word is the odd one out in each of the following sets of words? Allow yourself 9 minutes to complete this test.

1

a large

b big

c small

d enormous

e massive

2

a immodest

b improper

c offensive

d indecent

e modest

3

a seats

b onlookers

c viewers

d audience

e spectators

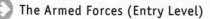

4

a hesitant

b reluctant

c tentative

d decisive

e uncertain

5

a return

b departure

c reappear

d revert

e regress

6

a fatigued

b drowsy

c lively

d tired

e weary

7

a industrious

b diligent

c lazy

d tireless

e busy

8

a　confusion

b　bedlam

c　disorder

d　chaos

e　order

9

a　ordered

b　chronological

c　consecutive

d　random

e　sequential

10

a　alterable

b　inflexible

c　adaptable

d　changeable

e　adjustable

11

a　recover

b　rescue

c　save

d　salvage

e　capture

12

a impertinent
b impudent
c respectful
d discourteous
e rude

13

a gloom
b amusement
c fun
d laughter
e conviviality

14

a tyrannical
b just
c despotic
d repressive
e dictatorial

15

a decipher
b muddle
c scramble
d distort
e jumble

16

a warranty

b endorsement

c insurance

d security

e uncertain

17

a gross

b aggregate

c whole

d net

e total

18

a counterfeit

b genuine

c sham

d fraud

e fake

19

a flimsy

b heavy

c thin

d fine

e delicate

20

a   unintentional

b   fortuitous

c   deliberate

d   accidental

e   unexpected

21

a   jubilee

b   anniversary

c   festival

d   party

e   balloons

22

a   universal

b   narrow

c   liberal

d   broad

e   wide

23

a   indifference

b   obsession

c   passion

d   fixation

e   crush

24

a   carefree

b   lively

c   depressed

d   perky

e   breezy

25

a   reckless

b   wary

c   rash

d   impetuous

e   heedless

26

a   journalist

b   author

c   reader

d   writer

e   novelist

27

a   baby

b   junior

c   infant

d   child

e   adult

28

a defend

b safeguard

c preserve

d destroy

e protect

29

a lass

b spinster

c dame

d widow

e bachelor

30

a fictional

b factual

c literary

d imagined

e invented

Answers on page 148.

Navy Test 3

NUMERACY

Solve the following problems without using a calculator.
Allow yourself 16 minutes.

1　A car averages 45 miles per hour. How far will it have travelled in four hours?

a　180 miles

b　142 miles

c　90 miles

d　160 miles

e　170 miles

2　A family spends £168 per month on food. How much will they spend on food in a year?

a　£168

b　£2800

c　£1416

d　£2016

e　£1916

3　What is 20% of 400?

a　50

b　320

c　90

d　80

e　100

4 If a snack costs £3.99, how much would five of them cost?

a £21.95

b £20.00

c £19.95

d £19.99

e £19.00

5 A quarter of the applicants for a job were female. If there were 120 applicants, how many were female?

a 35

b 20

c 90

d 100

e 30

6 How much would the interest on a loan of £1000 for one year be if the interest rate is 5%?

a £50

b £5

c £100

d £55

e £500

7   A third of a company's 660 employees are over 40. How many is this?

a   300

b   440

c   220

d   200

e   60

8   Express ⅖ as a percentage.

a   20%

b   40%

c   25%

d   15%

e   45%

9   If the average weekly wage is £420 but a worker earns only half of this, how much does he earn?

a   £190

b   £220

c   £200

d   £400

e   £210

10 There were 123 uniforms in the store but a third have been given out. How many remain?

a 41

b 82

c 60

d 83

e 63

11 What is 25% discount on an item costing £37.60?

a £10.00

b £9.40

c £10.40

d £8.49

e £3.76

12 If five out of ten workers drive to work, what percentage does not drive to work?

a 30%

b 20%

c 40%

d 50%

e 55%

13 What is 15% of 80?

a 100

b 12

c 95

d 10

e 50

14 If a working day is eight hours, how many hours will have been worked by three people in two days?

a 16

b 50

c 48

d 54

e 24

15 Work out 0.55 + 4.6.

a 4.05

b 51.5

c 5.5

d 5.0

e 5.15

16 A discount of 10% is offered on a car costing £12,500. What is the discounted price?

a £1250

b £11,250

c £11,200

d £12,000

e £11,500

17 If you work eight out of 24 hours, what fraction of the day do you work?

a ⅙

b ½

c ¼

d ⅓

e ⅕

18 What is 0.2 expressed as a fraction?

a ⅙

b ½

c ⅒

d ¼

e ⅕

19 What is one-third of 420?

a 150

b 140

c 120

d 160

e 280

20 One spare part for a car costs £12.90. How much would 100 of these parts cost?

a £1290

b £129

c £12,900

d £129.90

e £1290.90

21 If your restaurant bill comes to £45.00 and you decide to add a 10% tip, how much would you pay in total?

a £49.50

b £49.00

c £50.00

d £40.50

e £52.00

22 If you earn £20,000, pay £2500 in tax and £1400 for National Insurance, what would your net pay be?

a £17,000

b £20,000

c £16,000

d £16,100

e £17,500

23 You have a standard 40-hour working week. If you work one hour of overtime each day from Monday to Thursday and half an hour on Friday, how many hours would you work in total?

a 44

b 45

c 44.5

d 45.5

e 42.5

24 If you walk at 4 mph for three-quarters of an hour, how far would you have walked?

a 5 miles

b 4 miles

c 1 mile

d 3 miles

e 2 miles

25 If you spend £12.65 in a shop and pay with a £20 note, how much change would you receive?

a £7.25

b £8.25

c £8.35

d £7.55

e £7.35

26 If you buy a PC costing £499.00 and four games costing £12 each, how much would you have spent in total?

a £549

b £523

c £547

d £548

e £524

27 At an average speed of 40 mph, how long would it take for you to drive 200 miles?

a 5 hours 30 minutes

b 5 hours

c 4 hours

d 3 hours

e 6 hours

28 What is 0.90 expressed as a fraction?

a 9/10

b 9.00

c 1/10

d 1/6

e 3/4

29 What percentage of £64.00 is £16.00?

a 20%

b 25%

c 1/4

d 30%

e 40%

30 If a test has 30 questions and each one takes an average of 30 seconds, how long would it take you to complete the test?

a 1 hour

b 30 minutes.

c 15 minutes

d 45 minutes

e 10 minutes

Answers on page 149.

Navy Test 4

MECHANICAL COMPREHENSION

Answer the following questions. Allow yourself 10 minutes.

1 What is usually used to make holes in wood or metal?

a a drill

b a screwdriver

c a hammer

d a wrench

e a pair of pliers

2 What changes the amount that a bicycle moves forward with each pedal stroke?

a electric power

b pedals

c wheels

d gears

e wind

3 What sort of bridge has cables, ropes or chains strung across the gap to be bridged?

a a low bridge

b a high bridge

c a beam bridge

d an arch bridge

e a suspension bridge

4 What is used to smelt iron?

a a blast furnace

b a Bunsen burner

c a gas fire

d a water cooling tower

e an oil rig

5 Which of these items of equipment would be part of an oil rig?

a a chandelier

b a car wash

c a derrick

d a backhoe

e an escalator

6 On what sort of fire would water best be used as an extinguisher?

a flammable liquids

b wood and paper

c electrical

d dry chemicals

e liquid chemicals

7 What is used to control temperature in an immersion heater?

a a heating element

b a thermostat

c water

d an insulation jacket

e a drain valve

8 What device in a washing machine prevents dirty water being sucked back into the water supply?

a the gearbox

b a solenoid

c an anti-siphon device

d the motor

e the pump

9 What creates suction inside a vacuum cleaner?

a a porous bag

b the brush mechanism

c a fan

d a rise in pressure

e a drop in pressure

10 Which of these would be heavier?

a a kilo of potatoes

b a kilo of feathers

c a kilo of water

d a kilo of lead

e none of these

11 What unit is used to measure force?

a ohm

b ampere

c Newton

d volt

e tension

12 What instrument measures atmospheric pressure?

a a barometer

b a thermometer

c a ruler

d a theodolyte

e a speedometer

13 What does perpendicular mean?

a deep

b weak

c unstable

d at right angles

e high

14 When you are undoing nuts, what would give you greater turning effect?

a your fingers

b a pair of pliers

c a spanner

d grease

e friction

15 Which of these helps to keep a car stable?

a low centre of gravity

b a narrow wheel base

c a high centre of gravity

d high speed

e low speed

16 What is the opposite of acceleration?

a speed

b deceleration

c movement

d force

e ascension

17 What would a trainer usually use to time an athlete?

a   a clock

b   the finishing line

c   his judgement

d   a tape measure

e   a stopwatch

18 What is mixed with fuel in a rocket to make it burn?

a   water

b   air

c   oxygen

d   nitrogen

e   hydrogen

19 What is the unit of measurement for work?

a   joule

b   force

c   volt

d   Newton

e   mass

20 In woodworking, what sort of tool would most help you to construct a perfect corner?

a   a screwdriver

b   a workbench

c   a reciprocating saw

d   a hammer

e   a mitre box

21 Which of these devices would multiply a force to allow you to lift a heavy load using less effort?

a   a motor

b   a lever

c   an engine

d   a wheel

e   a pedal

22 What generates energy in a solar power panel?

a   the sun

b   the moon

c   air

d   wind

e   movement

23 How many cylinders do most petrol engine cars have?

a   1

b   2

c   3

d   4

e   none

24 What substance in a thermometer expands when heated to register temperature?

a water

b dye

c mercury

d oxygen

e glass

25 Which of these is the best conductor of heat?

a water

b wool

c air

d fat

e copper

26 How many mirrors do you need to make a periscope?

a 4

b 3

c 1

d 2

e none

27 What is the area around a magnet called?

a force

b magnetic field

c magnetic object

d a compass

e the poles

28 What device allows you to change the voltage of a current supply?

a a voltmeter

b a primary circuit

c a secondary circuit

d a transformer

e an ammeter

29 How many grams in a kilogram?

a 10

b 100

c 1000

d 10,000

e 500

30 What is the force in a stretched material?

a resistance

b tension

c friction

d expansion

e thrust

Answers on page 150.

SECTION 3 – THE AIR FORCE

Air Force Test 1

VERBAL REASONING

In this test you are given some written information then asked questions that test your ability to understand, interpret and use this information. Allow yourself 15 minutes.

A car showroom has the following models on display:

Car A is red, a hatchback and seats up to five people.

Car B is a blue saloon car has a tow bar and seats up to six people.

Car C is metallic blue, has a top speed of 110 mph and seats six people.

Car D is red, has a top speed of 120 mph, is convertible and will not seat more than four people.

Car E is black saloon model with alloy wheels and seats up to five people.

Which car would each of the following choose:

1   A family of five who want to tow a caravan and don't like red cars.

a   Car A

b   Car B

c   Car C

d   Car D

e   Car E

2 A family of four who like hatchback cars but not metallic paint.

a Car A

b Car B

c Car C

d Car D

e Car E

3 A single man who prefers saloon cars, doesn't need a tow bar and does not want metallic paint.

a Car A

b Car B

c Car C

d Car D

e Car E

4 A middle-aged couple who sometimes need to put a wheelchair in the boot for one of their parents.

a Car A

b Car B

c Car C

d Car D

e Car E

5   A family of four who prefer a metallic paint finish.

a   Car A

b   Car B

c   Car C

d   Car D

e   Car E

Three friends have decided to go to the theatre together. Bill enjoys musicals but will go to any live performance. Sita prefers Shakespeare's plays or will go to see any dramas but prefers not to go out at night. Declan does not like musicals or comedies – he prefers serious plays but his first choice would not be Shakespeare.

They check the listings and see that their choices are as follows:

a   A Shakespearian tragedy at 7.30 pm.

b   A comedy play at 2.30 or 7.30 pm.

c   A light-hearted musical at 3.00 pm.

d   A gritty drama at 2.30 or 7.30 pm.

e   A Shakespearian comedy at 2.30 or 7.00 pm.

6   Which would be Bill's first choice?

a   The Shakespearian tragedy

b   The comedy play

c   The musical

d   The drama

e   The Shakespearian comedy

7   Which would be Sita's first choice?

a   The Shakespearian tragedy

b   The comedy play

c   The musical

d   The drama

e   The Shakespearian comedy

8   Which would be Declan's first choice?

a   The Shakespearian tragedy

b   The comedy play

c   The musical

d   The drama

e   The Shakespearian comedy

9   Which choice would Sita like to see but cannot because it does not have a matinee performance?

a   The Shakespearian tragedy

b   The comedy play

c   The musical

d   The drama

e   The Shakespearian comedy

10 Which choice would suit all of them?

a The Shakespearian tragedy

b The comedy play

c The musical

d The drama

e The Shakespearian comedy

Nelson works for a large multi-national company and usually drives to work but frequently goes abroad by air on business. His friend, John, works for the same company but, as he works in the Accounts Department, does not have any cause for travel for work. As he does not drive, he takes the train to work. Niamh works in a cake shop and walks to work. Her husband, Steve, is a car mechanic and drives their car to work. Steve's father, Fred, is retired.

11 Who usually takes a train to work?

a Nelson

b John

c Niamh

d Steve

e Fred

12 Who does not go out to work?

a Nelson

b John

c Niamh

d Steve

e Fred

13 Whose job involves foreign travel?

a Nelson

b John

c Niamh

d Steve

e Fred

14 Who walks to work?

a Nelson

b John

c Niamh

d Steve

e Fred

15 Who always drives to work?

a Nelson

b John

c Niamh

d Steve

e Fred

Use this table of information to answer the next five questions:

LENGTH OF SERVICE					
	Departments				
Staff Members	**Sales**	**Accounts**	**Customer Service**	**Maintenance**	**Manufacturing**
Peter		20 years			
Karen	1 year		6 years		
Meena		15 years*			
David	2 years				1 year
Sean				4 years	

* NB This is not continuous service. Meena left after three years but returned to work for the company.

16 Which two members of staff have worked in more than one department?

a Peter and Karen

b Karen and David

c David and Sean

d Sean and Peter

e Karen and Peter

17 Who has the longest service with the company?

a Peter

b Karen

c Meena

d David

e Sean

18 Which two members of staff will have received awards for continuous service of ten years or more?

a Peter and Karen

b Karen and David

c David and Sean

d Sean and Peter

e Peter and Meena

19 Who has seven years service in total?

a Peter

b Karen

c Meena

d David

e Sean

20 Which department has the longest serving member of staff?

a Sales

b Accounts

c Customer Service

d Maintenance

e Manufacturing

Answers on page 151.

Air Force Test 2

NUMERICAL REASONING PART 1

Solve the following without using a calculator. Allow yourself 4 minutes.

1 Calculate 0.2×5

a 2.0

b 1.0

c 1.5

d 0.5

e 0.10

2 Calculate $65 \div 5$

a 14

b 15

c 10

d 12

e 13

3 Work out 3 + 0.5 + 7.6

a 12.6

b 12.1

c 10.1

d 11.1

e 11.0

4 Take 29 away from 43

a 15

b 14

c 16

d 13

e 24

5 Work out 0.1 × 12

a 120

b 0.012

c 1.2

d 12

e 0.12

6 Calculate ⅓ + ½

a ⅚

b 1

c ⅔

d ⅙

e 1⅙

7 Calculate 12 ÷ 0.2

a 40

b 120

c 60

d 50

e 48

8 Work out 175 ÷ 7

a 49

b 27

c 36

d 26

e 25

9 What is 14 − 0.2 + 23?

a 46.8

b 28.6

c 36.8

d 38.6

e 37.2

10 Calculate 25 ÷ ½

a 20

b 5

c 50

d 100

e 12.5

11 Calculate 18 ÷ 0.5

a 180

b 360

c 27

d 36

e 72

12 Find ⅖ of 120

a 50

b 48

c 40

d 44

e 42

Answers on page 151.

Air Force Test 3

NUMERICAL REASONING PART 2

Use the information in the graphs and tables to answer the questions. Allow yourself 11 minutes.

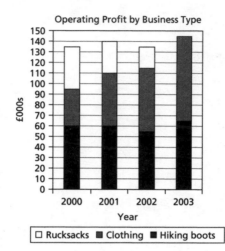

Operating Profit by Business Type

□ Rucksacks ■ Clothing ■ Hiking boots

1 In 2003 no Rucksacks were produced. How much extra profit did Clothing make in this year compared with the previous year.

a £60,000

b £20,000

c £55,000

d £65,000

e £80,000

2 What was the total operating profit in 2001?

a £120,000

b £130,000

c £135,000

d £140,000

e £145,000

3 How much operating profit was made on Rucksacks in 2000?

a £50,000

b £60,000

c £40,000

d £135,000

e £35,000

4 Which year was the most profitable for the department producing Clothing?

a 2000

b 2001

c 2002

d 2003

e Cannot tell

5 What was the total operating profit made over the four years by the Rucksacks department?

a £90,000

b £80,000

c £70,000

d £60,000

e £50,000

Two groups of people – over 35s and under 35s – were asked what sort of television programme they most liked to watch. The pie charts illustrate the results. Answer the questions using the information in the charts.

Chart 1 Viewers under 35

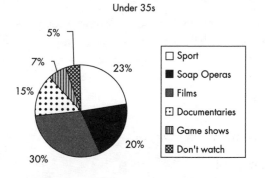

Under 35s

Total viewers under 35 surveyed = 200

Chart 2 Viewers over 35

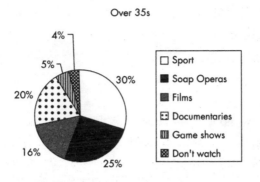

Over 35s

4%
5%
20%
16%
25%
30%

☐ Sport
■ Soap Operas
▤ Films
⊞ Documentaries
▥ Game shows
▩ Don't watch

Total viewers over 35 surveyed = 300

6 How many people in total (over and under 35s) said their favourite type of TV programme was Soap Operas?

a 45

b 105

c 115

d 100

e 110

7 How many over 35s prefer Sport?

a 136

b 110

c 100

d 30

e 90

8 How many people in total don't watch TV?

a 22

b 12

c 9

d 20

e 18

9 How many more under 35s than over 35s prefer Films?

a 30

b 18

c 12

d 14

e 16

10 How many under 35s prefer either Soap Operas or Sport?

a 100

b 46

c 43

d 86

e 40

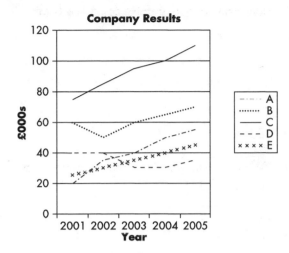

Use the information shown in the graph to answer the following questions.

11 Which of the five companies had the greatest increase in profit between 2001 and 2002?

a Company A

b Company B

c Company C

d Company D

e Company E

12 What was the total profit of all five companies in 2005?

a £260,000

b £300

c £300,000

d £315,000

e £315

13 Which company had the biggest increase in profit between 2004 and 2005?

a Company A

b Company B

c Company C

d Company D

e Company E

14 Only one company suffered a fall in profit between 2001 and 2002. By how much did that company's profit decrease?

a £10,000

b £100,000

c £50,000

d £60,000

e £10

15 By how much did Company C's profit differ from that of Company A in 2001?

a £75,000

b £55,000

c £50,000

d £50

e £55

Answers on page 152.

Air Force Test 4

WORK RATE

In this test you must identify alternative codes. You are given a grid with four columns and in each column there is a letter, a number and a symbol. For each question you are given an original code made up of three letters, three numbers or three symbols, each taken from a separate column. For each of the items in this original code there are two alternative items in the same column. Your task is to choose, from the answers given, the alternative code that comprises items taken from the same column and in the same order as the original code. Allow yourself 4 minutes.

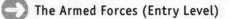

1 Which could be an alternative code for 293?

A	D	W	Q
3	5	2	9
□	●	∇	◆

a W□∇

b □◆9

c W◆A

d ∇◆Q

e DW□

2 Which could be an alternative code for PQR?

P	Q	R	M
4	8	5	2
●	∇	◆	□

a M□5

b 4∇5

c PV●

d 2◆8

e ◆52

3 Which could be an alternative code for 297?

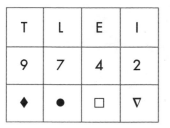

T	L	E	I
9	7	4	2
♦	●	□	▽

a T♦2

b IE□

c ▽T●

d L●□

e ET●

4 Which could be an alternative code for 246?

J	H	F	R
7	4	2	6
●	□	♦	▽

a F●♦

b H□●

c F♦J

d R□●

e ♦HR

5   Which could be an alternative code for RUN?

U	N	W	R
5	3	6	2
♦	□	●	∇

a   ∇53

b   W6□

c   26∇

d   ∇♦6

e   ●∇3

6   Which could be an alternative code for RVB?

B	V	R	Q
7	8	9	3
□	♦	∇	●

a   8♦□

b   7∇●

c   B●♦

d   ∇8□

e   3●B

7 Which could be an alternative code for 359?

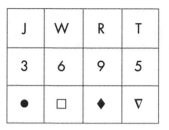

J	W	R	T
3	6	9	5
●	□	◆	▽

a RT●

b ▽●W

c J●◆

d ●▽R

e □JR

8 Which could be an alternative code for UMN?

U	Y	M	N
7	4	3	9
◆	□	▽	●

a ●34

b ◆▽9

c 39●

d 4▽7

e □43

9 Which could be an alternative code for 654?

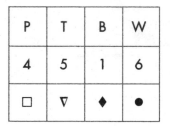

P	T	B	W
4	5	1	6
□	∇	◆	●

a W1□

b □◆B

c W∇P

d T●P

e ●BP

10 Which could be an alternative code for FSL?

H	F	L	S
7	5	8	3
∇	□	◆	●

a □●8

b □◆3

c ∇58

d 73◆

e 85●

11 Which could be an alternative code for 234?

T	P	Q	E
6	3	2	4
∇	◆	□	●

a   ∇●E

b   Q□P

c   Q◆E

d   PQ●

e   □PT

12 Which could be an alternative code for RNM?

N	M	B	R
9	7	4	2
∇	●	□	◆

a   29●

b   ◆□9

c   4□∇

d   27∇

e   □92

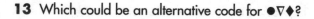
13 Which could be an alternative code for ●∇◆?

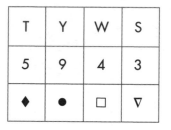

T	Y	W	S
5	9	4	3
◆	●	□	∇

a W49

b ST9

c 9W3

d YS9

e Y3T

14 Which could be an alternative code for SOP?

P	O	W	S
7	5	4	1
□	◆	●	∇

a 14□

b 15□

c ●◆7

d ∇47

e 1∇5

15 Which could be an alternative code for 289?

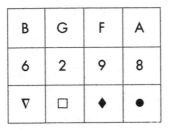

B	G	F	A
6	2	9	8
▽	□	◆	●

a   G●□

b   □BF

c   ▽□B

d   □AF

e   B●▽

16 Which could be an alternative code for HKY?

Y	D	H	K
5	3	1	9
●	▽	◆	□

a   91●

b   ▽95

c   ◆□9

d   □●3

e   19●

17 Which could be an alternative code for 345?

P	I	Q	T
6	4	5	3
∇	□	◆	●

a T□P

b TI◆

c ∇□Q

d ●◆□

e TIP

18 Which could be an alternative code for FAB?

B	Z	A	F
3	5	7	9
□	∇	●	◆

a ◆5□

b ∇79

c 9●□

d 795

e 97∇

19 Which could be an alternative code for HGS?

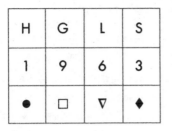

H	G	L	S
1	9	6	3
●	□	∇	♦

a ●□3

b 1□6

c ●6♦

d 391

e □●∇

20 Which could be an alternative code for 246?

J	G	V	M
4	2	6	8
♦	∇	●	□

a MJV

b ∇●♦

c ∇VM

d GM●

e G♦V

Answers on page 152.

Air Force Test 5

SPATIAL REASONING PART 1

In each question you are given three shapes. Each of the shapes will have at least one side labelled with a letter – x or y. Imagine you must make another, larger shape from these shapes by putting together the sides with the same letter. You must decide, from the choices given in the answers, what these shapes will look like when they are put together with the sides marked with the same letters next to each other. Allow yourself 4 minutes.

1

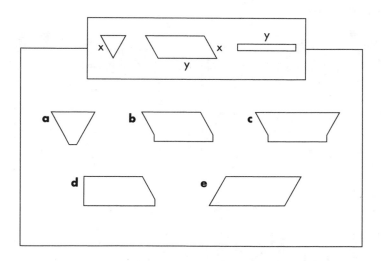

2

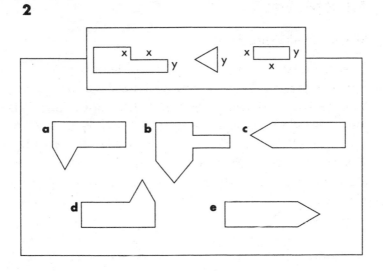

3

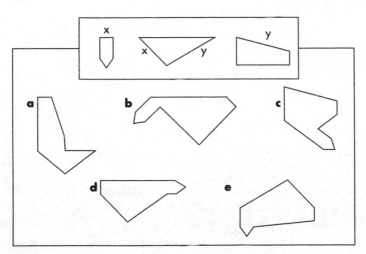

4

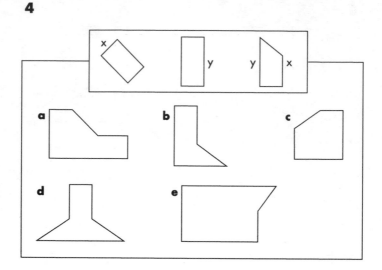

5

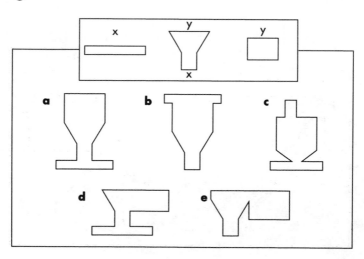

6

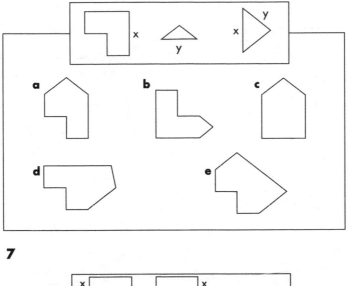

7

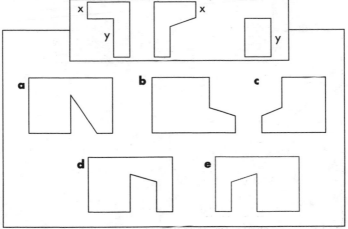

8

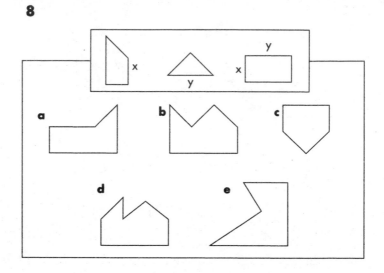

9

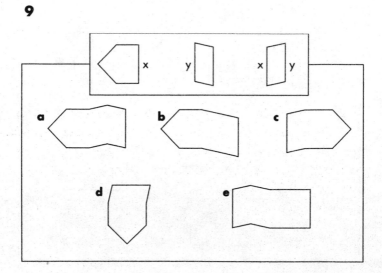

10

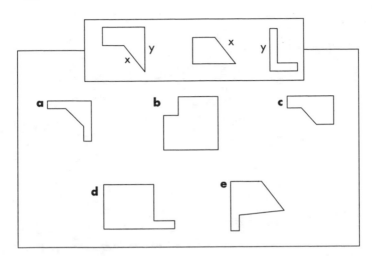

Answers on page 153.

Air Force Test 6

SPATIAL REASONING PART 2

In each question you are shown two three-dimensional objects, each with a dot placed in one corner. You must decide, from the choices given, which option shows the same objects rotated and with the dot placed in the correct corner.

Allow yourself 3 minutes.

1

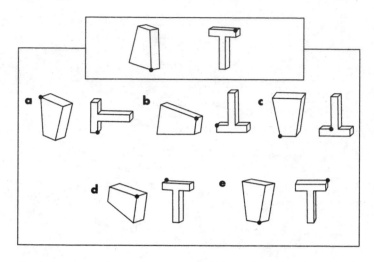

2

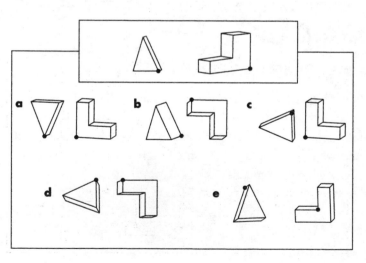

3

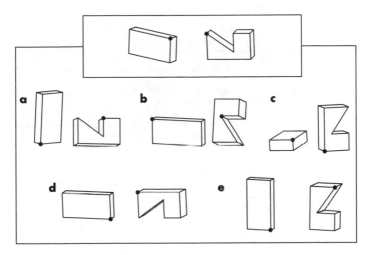

4

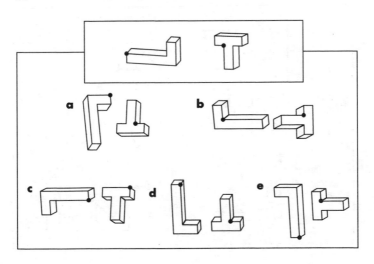

5

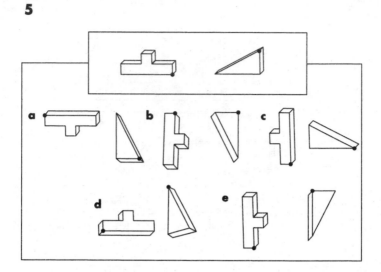

6

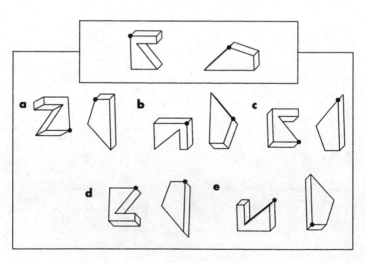

7

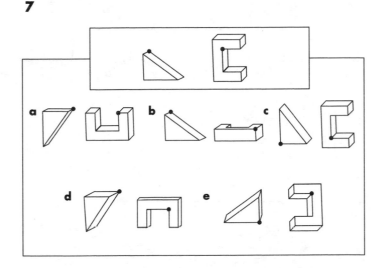

8

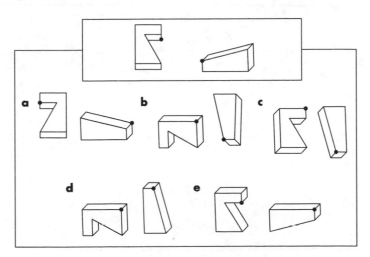

9

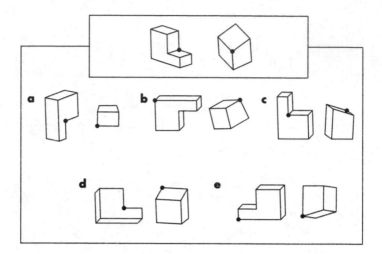

10

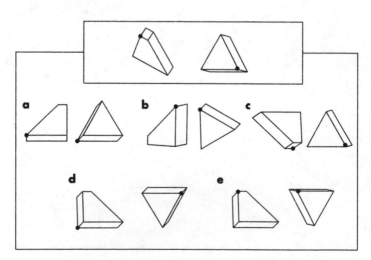

Answers on page 153.

Air Force Test 7

ELECTRICAL COMPREHENSION

Here you are asked questions to test your knowledge of basic electrical concepts. Allow yourself 11 minutes.

1 Ohm's Law is used to calculate:

a radiation

b conduction

c resistance

d temperature

e power

2 What would you use to measure electric current?

a an ammeter

b a lamp

c a resistor

d a transistor

e a plug

3 What is an electrical circuit called where the current passes through one thing after another?

a a complex circuit

b a simple circuit

c a series circuit

d a progressive circuit

e a timed circuit

4 If a lamp 'blows' on a series circuit, what happens to the remaining lamps?

a they burn brighter

b they all go out

c nothing

d they catch fire

e they use more electricity

5 What type of circuits are normally used in houses?

a single circuits

b series circuits

c parallel circuits

d coextensive circuits

e matching circuits

6 In parallel circuits, how does the current passing into a junction compare with the current passing out of that same junction?

a it is smaller

b it is more powerful

c it is less powerful

d it is greater

e it is the same

7 What is 'amps' short for?

a amplifiers

b amplitude

c amphibians

d amperes

e ampersands

8 What three things can electricity be used to provide?

a light, fuel and power

b water, ice and speed

c heat, movement and light

d controls, switches and power

e warmth, heat and cold

9 We generate electricity when:

a a chemical reaction takes place

b a button is pressed

c the mains supply is connected

d the temperature rises

e the temperature falls

10 What would happen to a motor if armature resistance is increased so that less current passes?

a it would speed up

b it would get hot

c it would continue at the same rate

d it would slow down

e it would use more power

11 What is used in a volume control circuit in a radio?

a a series resistor

b a variable resistor

c a temperature control

d a low voltage meter

e a volt meter

12 What unit of measurement refers to resistance?

a volts

b amps

c Celsius

d Fahrenheit

e ohms

13 What is a diode used for?

a to produce a direct current

b to measure resistance

c to control the temperature

d to measure voltage

e to change the temperature

14 What is a joulemeter used for?

a to change the direction of the current

b to measure energy provided from a power supply

c to control the flow of current

d to measure resistance

e to provide power

15 What is power measured in?

a seconds

b degrees

c centigrade

d watts

e ohms

16 Through which wire in an electric cable would no current normally pass?

a earth

b copper

c live

d glass

e neutral

17 What colour is the live wire in an electric cable?

a yellow and green

b red and blue

c purple

d blue

e brown

18 What protects wiring against overloading?

a insulation

b a fuse

c water

d the wire breaks

e the neutral wire

19 Why is an earthing lead used during aircraft refuelling?

a   it reduces odour

b   it allows charge to pass safely to earth

c   it makes the fuel transfer quicker

d   it connects it to the onboard computer

e   it provides power

20 What switches off the current in an oven or an immersion heater when the correct temperature has been reached?

a   a thermostat

b   a fuse

c   a timer

d   an earth wire

e   a circuit breaker

21 Why should a hairdryer's air inlet not be covered up?

a   it would blow only cold air

b   the air blown would get too hot

c   there would be no resistance

d   it needs a large air flow

e   it would use more energy

Answers on page 153.

Air Force Test 8

MECHANICAL COMPREHENSION

Answer the following questions about mechanical concepts. Allow yourself 10 minutes.

1 How many millimetres in a metre?

a 10

b 100

c 1000

d 10,000

e 100,000

2 Why is steel a common building material?

a it is bendy

b it is strong

c it can be painted any colour

d it is light

e it is heavy

3 What would be used to reduce friction by allowing surfaces to roll over each other?

a glass fibre

b wheels

c water

d gravity

e ball bearings

4   Which of these objects has the advantage of high pressure at one end and low pressure at the other?

a   a football

b   a drawing pin

c   a coat hanger

d   a concrete post

e   a pillow

5   How might an engineer describe cast iron?

a   flexible

b   brittle

c   weak

d   elastic

e   unbreakable

6   What is the line on a boat called which shows the lowest level that the boat should be allowed to sink?

a   the sea line

b   the loading line

c   the shipping line

d   the Plimsoll line

e   the Maginot line

7 Whose law of motion states that for every force there is an equal and opposite force?

a Darwin's

b Newton's

c Murphy's

d Boyle's

e Smith's

8 If an object is allowed to fall freely, what happens to the speed of its fall as it approaches the ground?

a deceleration

b acceleration

c stays the same

d it varies

e cannot tell

9 What word describes a fluid's resistance to flow?

a turbulence

b pressure

c flow rate

d solidity

e viscosity

10 What sort of energy does food have?

a strain energy

b kinetic energy

c chemical energy

d light energy

e pure energy

11 What sort of force would produce heat?

a strain

b wheels

c a pulley

d efficiency

e friction

12 What two things do you need to know to calculate momentum?

a weight and force

b speed and direction

c direction and weight

d mass and velocity

e speed and weight

13 What is the inward force called that causes an object to move in a circle?

a   centripetal

b   velocity

c   speed

d   magnetism

e   mass

14 What happens to the pressure in a liquid as you go deeper into it?

a   it decreases

b   it gets denser

c   it gets lighter

d   it is not affected

e   it increases

15 What transmits the pressure in a hydraulic jack?

a   water

b   oil

c   the piston

d   the cylinder

e   the output force

16 What are the chemicals used in refrigerators called?

a kinetic gases

b bleach

c freons

d water

e air

17 What heats up and completes the electrical circuit in a fire alarm?

a a bimetallic strip

b the battery

c a heating element

d a thermostat

e smoke

18 Through what can heat NOT be transferred by convection?

a liquids

b solids

c air

d steam

e gases

19 In a radio system, what separates out the radio and audio frequencies and decodes the signal?

a a demodulator

b a modulator

c an aerial

d a transmitter

e an amplifier

20 What is produced when a plucked string vibrates?

a a signal

b tension

c sound

d heat

e oxygen

Answers on page 154.

Air Force Test 9

MEMORY PART 1

There are two parts to the memory test, both of which are presented on film in the actual test and both of which consist of 10 questions. The speed at which you work will be determined by the film but you should try to work quickly and accurately.

You will be shown a sequence of between six and eight letters, which will appear on screen one at a time. You must remember the order in which they appear. You will then be shown two letters from the sequence and you must decide how many letters were between them in the sequence.

Remembering that in the actual test the numbers will be shown on screen one at a time, study the following sequences of letters by uncovering them one by one, then answer the question that follows.

1 Y   K   L   P   E   S   Q   C

How many letters were shown between L and C?

a 3

b 4

c 5

d 0

2 A   C   D   X   Y   L

How many letters were shown between A and D?

a 2

b 3

c 1

d 4

3 S   P   O   F   L   Y   N

How many letters were shown between S and Y?

a 4

b 3

c 2

d 0

4 B   N   M   F   S   T   L   P

How many letters were shown between S and T?

a   1

b   0

c   2

d   3

5 X   L   Y   T   N   D

How many letters were shown between L and T?

a   4

b   3

c   2

d   1

6 M   N   Q   R   O   D   B

How many letters were shown between R and B?

a   3

b   1

c   0

d   2

7 C   N   Y   S   L   K   O   P

How many letters were shown between N and O?

a   4

b   3

c   2

d   1

8 T   L   N   F   X   M

How many letters were shown between F and M?

a 4

b 3

c 2

d 1

9 R   G   X   F   T   S   O   L

How many letters were shown between X and S?

a 4

b 3

c 2

d 1

10 C   K   L   M   B   W   N

How many letters were shown between K and B?

a 4

b 3

c 2

d 1

Answers on page 155.

Air Force Test 10

MEMORY PART 2

In this part of the on-screen memory test you will be shown a set of either two or three grids each containing a pattern within the squares in the grid. You must remember where the pattern is in each grid and then you must select, from the choices given, the answer that represents how the pattern would appear if the grids were combined. In the actual test the grids will be presented on film, one after the other.

1

 a

b

 c

d

2

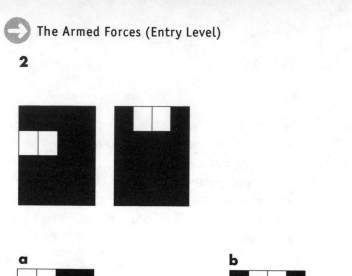

a

b

c

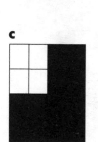

d

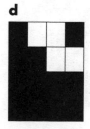

3

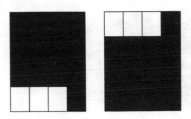

a

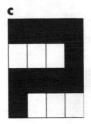

b

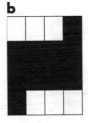

c

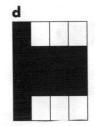

d

4

a

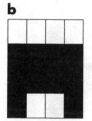

b

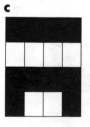

c

d

5

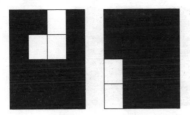

a

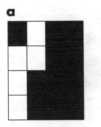

b

c

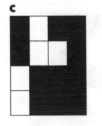

d

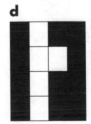

6

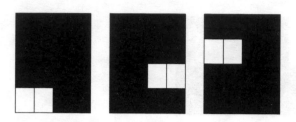

a

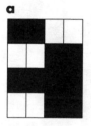

b

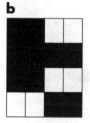

c

d

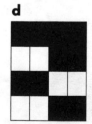

7

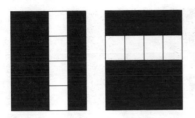

a

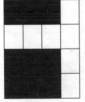

b

c

d

8

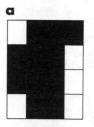 

a

b

c

d

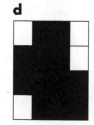

9

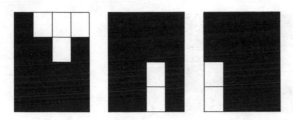

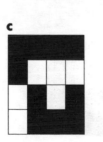

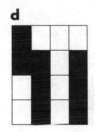

10

a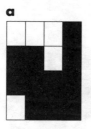

b

c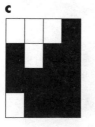

d

Answers on page 155.

CHAPTER 3

Answers to tests

SECTION 1 – THE ARMY

Army Test 1   (from page 19)

REASONING

1 b Sam	**11 a** Colin
2 b John	**12 a** Pat
3 b Sue	**13 b** Fred
4 b Andrew	**14 b** Millie
5 b Barbara	**15 b** Michael
6 a Fiona	**16 a** Diane
7 b John	**17 b** Olivia
8 b Kate	**18 a** Carl
9 b Bob	**19 a** Bob
10 b Betty	**20 a** Zoë

Army Test 2 (from page 23)

LETTER CHECKING

1	**d** 3	11	**a** 0
2	**e** 4	12	**d** 3
3	**a** 0	13	**c** 2
4	**b** 1	14	**c** 2
5	**c** 2	15	**b** 1
6	**e** 4	16	**d** 3
7	**c** 2	17	**a** 0
8	**d** 3	18	**c** 2
9	**e** 4	19	**c** 2
10	**c** 2	20	**c** 2

Army Test 3 (from page 30)

NUMBER DISTANCE

1	**c** 7	9	**a** 3
2	**c** 20	10	**c** 8
3	**b** 14	11	**b** 3
4	**c** 11	12	**c** 19
5	**c** 3	13	**a** 17
6	**b** 18	14	**c** 2
7	**a** 14	15	**c** 19
8	**a** 7	16	**a** 2

17 **c** 11   **19** **c** 1

18 **b** 15   **20** **b** 20

Army Test 4   (from page 35)

ODD ONE OUT

1 **b** bus   **11** **a** camera

2 **a** common   **12** **c** chair

3 **b** also   **13** **a** meet

4 **c** drastic   **14** **b** pullover

5 **a** seven   **15** **a** fall

6 **a** dry   **16** **c** furniture

7 **b** picture   **17** **a** sky

8 **c** cooperate   **18** **a** careful

9 **a** devious   **19** **b** temper

10 **c** evening   **20** **c** star

Army Test 5   (from page 39)

SYMBOL ROTATION

1 **b** 1   **6** **c** 2

2 **c** 2   **7** **b** 1

3 **a** 0   **8** **a** 0

4 **c** 2   **9** **b** 1

5 **b** 1   **10** **c** 2

SECTION 2 – THE NAVY

Navy Test 1   (from page 43)

VERBAL LOGICAL REASONING TEST

1	**d** week		**16**	**c** loss
2	**b** drink		**17**	**a** football
3	**e** initial		**18**	**d** defect
4	**b** lemon		**19**	**b** get hitched
5	**a** poem		**20**	**b** pot
6	**b** ship		**21**	**a** compact disc
7	**b** day		**22**	**e** iron
8	**c** starter		**23**	**b** radio
9	**e** word		**24**	**c** still
10	**c** few		**25**	**d** farm
11	**a** confined		**26**	**b** oil
12	**d** walk		**27**	**e** beat
13	**a** hear		**28**	**b** boat
14	**d** library		**29**	**c** definition
15	**a** coward		**30**	**b** train

Navy Test 2   (from page 51)

ENGLISH LANGUAGE

1	**c** small		**4**	**d** decisive
2	**e** modest		**5**	**b** departure
3	**a** seats		**6**	**c** lively

7 **c** lazy

8 **e** order

9 **d** random

10 **b** inflexible

11 **e** capture

12 **c** respectful

13 **a** gloom

14 **b** just

15 **a** decipher

16 **e** uncertain

17 **d** net

18 **b** genuine

19 **b** heavy

20 **c** deliberate

21 **e** balloons

22 **b** narrow

23 **a** indifference

24 **c** depressed

25 **b** wary

26 **c** reader

27 **e** adult

28 **d** destroy

29 **e** bachelor

30 **b** factual

Navy Test 3   (from page 59)

NUMERACY

1 **a** 180 miles

2 **d** £2016

3 **d** 80

4 **c** £19.95

5 **e** 30

6 **a** 50

7 **c** 220

8 **b** 40%

9 **e** £210

10 **b** 82

11 **b** £9.40

12 **d** 50%

13 **b** 12

14 **c** 48

15 **e** 5.15

16 **b** £11,250

17 **d** ⅓

18 **e** ⅕

19 **b** 140

20 **a** £1290

21 **a** £49.50

22 **d** £16,100

23 **c** 44.5

24 **d** 3 miles

25 **e** £7.35

26 **c** £547

27 **b** 5 hours

28 **a** ‰

29 **b** 25%

30 **c** 15 minutes

Navy Test 4 (from page 69)

MECHANICAL COMPREHENSION

1 **a** a drill

2 **d** gears

3 **e** a suspension bridge

4 **a** a blast furnace

5 **c** a derrick

6 **b** wood and paper

7 **b** a thermostat

8 **c** an anti-siphon device

9 **e** a drop in pressure

10 **e** none of these

11 **c** Newton

12 **a** a barometer

13 **d** at right angles

14 **c** a spanner

15 **a** a low centre of gravity

16 **b** deceleration

17 **e** a stopwatch

18 **c** oxygen

19 **a** joule

20 **e** a mitre box

21 **b** a lever

22 **a** the sun

23 **d** 4

24 **c** mercury

25 **e** copper

26 **d** 2

27 **b** magnetic field

28 **d** a transformer

29 **c** 1000

30 **b** tension

SECTION 3 – THE AIR FORCE

Air Force Test 1   (from page 78)

VERBAL REASONING

1 **b** Car B

2 **a** Car A

3 **e** Car E

4 **a** Car A

5 **c** Car C

6 **c** The musical

7 **e** The Shakespearian comedy

8 **d** The drama

9 **a** The Shakespearian tragedy

10 **d** The drama

11 **b** John

12 **e** Fred

13 **a** Nelson

14 **c** Niamh

15 **d** Steve

16 **b** Karen and David

17 **a** Peter

18 **e** Peter and Meena

19 **b** Karen

20 **b** Accounts

Air Force Test 2   (from page 86)

NUMERICAL REASONING PART 1

1 **b** 1.0

2 **e** 13

3 **d** 11.1

4 **b** 14

5 **c** 1.2

6 **a** ⅝

7 **c** 60

8 **e** 25

9 **c** 36.8

10 **c** 50

11 **d** 36

12 **b** 48

Air Force Test 3 (from page 90)

NUMERICAL REASONING PART 2

1 b £20,000
2 d £140,000
3 c £40,000
4 d 2003
5 a £90,000
6 c 115
7 e 90
8 a 22

9 c 12
10 d 86
11 a Company A
12 d £315,000
13 c Company C
14 a £10,000
15 b £55,000

Air Force Test 4 (from page 97)

WORK RATE

1 c W♦A
2 b 4∇5
3 c ∇T●
4 e ♦HR
5 a ∇53
6 d ∇8□
7 d ●∇R
8 b ♦∇9
9 c W∇P
10 a □●8

11 c Q♦E
12 a 29●
13 e Y3T
14 b 15□
15 d □AF
16 e 19●
17 b T1♦
18 c 9●□
19 a ●□3
20 e G♦V

Air Force Test 5 (from page 108)

SPATIAL REASONING PART 1

1	c	**6**	d
2	e	**7**	e
3	b	**8**	b
4	a	**9**	a
5	a	**10**	d

Air Force Test 6 (from page 113)

SPATIAL REASONING PART 2

1	d	**6**	b
2	c	**7**	d
3	e	**8**	a
4	d	**9**	c
5	a	**10**	e

Air Force Test 7 (from page 119)

ELECTRICAL COMPREHENSION

1 c resistance		**5** c parallel circuits
2 a an ammeter		**6** e it is the same
3 c a series circuit		**7** d amperes
4 b they all go out		**8** c heat, movement and light

9 a a chemical reaction takes place

10 d it would slow down

11 b a variable resistor

12 e ohms

13 a to produce a low voltage direct current

14 b to measure energy provided from a power supply

15 d watts

16 a earth

17 e brown

18 b a fuse

19 b it allows charge to pass safely to earth

20 a a thermostat

21 d it needs a large air flow

Air Force Test 8   (from page 125)

MECHANICAL COMPREHENSION

1 c 1000

2 b it is strong

3 e ball bearings

4 b a drawing pin

5 b brittle

6 d Plimsoll line

7 b Newton's

8 b acceleration

9 e viscosity

10 c chemical energy

11 e friction

12 d mass and velocity

13 a centripetal

14 e it increases

15 b oil

16 c freons

17 a a bimetallic strip

18 b solids

19 a a demodulator

20 c sound

Air Force Test 9 (from page 131)

MEMORY PART 1

1 b 4	**6 d** 2
2 c 1	**7 a** 4
3 a 4	**8 d** 1
4 b 0	**9 c** 2
5 d 1	**10 c** 2

Air Force Test 10 (from page 135)

MEMORY PART 2

1 d	**6 d**
2 b	**7 c**
3 a	**8 a**
4 c	**9 d**
5 b	**10 b**

CHAPTER 4

Explanations of timed tests

You should note the correct answers in each type of test and, even if you have got that one right, read the accompanying explanation. This is where the common pitfalls will be demonstrated and tips given on how to avoid them. Where it would be impractical and repetitive to offer an explanation of each and every answer to a particular type of test, that explanation part will consist of a detailed description of how to tackle that sort of question together with some tips on how to avoid the pitfalls.

SECTION 1 – THE ARMY

Army Test 1

REASONING

This test assesses your ability to solve problems. To succeed at this test you should work steadily, concentrating on each individual question. Many of the sentences state the opposite to the questions that are asked. For instance, you may be asked 'Tom is brighter than Pete. Who is duller?' This can be confusing under test conditions so one tip to avoid this confusion is to restate the sentence in simple terms, making a statement about one of the people rather than making a comparison. For example, you could say to yourself 'Tom is brighter' and that might help you to answer the question 'Who is duller?' It will also often be particularly useful to restate a negative statement or question.

Remember that you will be completing this test on a computer screen. The question will not appear on the screen at the same time as the statement, so it will be necessary for you to memorise the statement.

Look at these few examples from the test so that you will be able to explain your answers to yourself.

1 The answer is **b** Sam. The statement given was 'Pete is taller than Sam' and the question you had to answer was 'Who is shorter?' If you ask yourself who is taller (Pete) it will be obvious to you that it is the other person in the statement who must be shorter i.e. Sam.

2 The answer is **b** John. Here the statement was that 'Norman arrived earlier than John' and the question you have to answer is 'Who arrived later?' If Norman was the earlier arrival of the two, then John must have arrived after him.

Now try question 6, which is stated in the negative:

The answer is **a** Fiona. In this question, the statement was 'Fiona is not as short as Ann' and the question was 'Who is taller?' Dealing with the negative in the statement and the different meaning in the question can be confusing so you will have to think clearly about your answer – and that is what the test is designed to test your ability to do, of course. Restate it as 'Ann is shorter', getting rid of the negative, and it will immediately become obvious that Fiona is the taller of the two.

Here is the full list of answers to Army Test 1:

1 The answer is **b** Sam

2 The answer is **b** John

3 The answer is **b** Sue

4 The answer is **b** Andrew

5 The answer is **b** Barbara

6 The answer is **a** Fiona

7 The answer is **b** John

8 The answer is **b** Kate

9 The answer is **b** Bob

10 The answer is **b** Betty

11 The answer is **a** Colin

12 The answer is **a** Pat

13 The answer is **b** Fred

14 The answer is **b** Millie

15 The answer is **b** Michael

16 The answer is **a** Diane

17 The answer is **b** Olivia

18 The answer is **a** Carl

19 The answer is **a** Bob

20 The answer is **a** Zoë

If you have encountered any problems in completing this test, you may need to work more slowly and carefully. Go through each of your answers and reason out, as shown above, exactly what the statement means and what you are being asked in the question. This will ensure success in this type of test. This test will run for 5 minutes and the number of questions you are asked in this time will depend on how quickly you are able to work.

Army Test 2

LETTER CHECKING

Here you are being tested to see how quickly and accurately you can perform checking tests in your head. Again, you should work steadily, and as accurately as possible. You could tackle this type of test by simply counting up the matching pairs as your eyes move across the boxes. Do not work too quickly until you have become familiar with the type of question – this leads to careless mistakes. Also, make sure that you count only matching pairs. In your haste you could count where there are matching letters but not in a pair. We will look at an example of this pitfall later.

This sort of test does not lend itself to individual explanations of all the questions. It should be sufficient for you to become familiar with what is required by going through just a few examples.

 The Armed Forces (Entry Level)

In question **1** the answer is **d** 3, i.e. there are three matching pairs shown.

Here is the question again:

a	f	g	x
A	L	G	X

The first pair a and A, the third pair g and G and the fourth pair x and X are matching but the second pair f and L are not the same, making three matching pairs.

In question **2** all the pairs are matching so the answer is **e** 4.

In question **3** we come up against a common error waiting to be made. Two of the letters on the top row are repeated on the bottom row – but unfortunately not as matching pairs and in fact there are no matching pairs in this question:

a	l	m	n
E	F	N	M

It doesn't help that the letters repeated on the bottom row are N and M – letters that are easy to mistake. The only solution to this type of pitfall is to work steadily and extremely carefully.

When you are doing the actual test on-screen, it will last for 4 minutes 15 seconds and, again, the number of questions you get the chance to answer will depend on your speed.

Here is the full list of answers to Army Test 2:

1 The answer is **d** 3

2 The answer is **e** 4

3 The answer is **a** 0

4 The answer is **b** 1

5 The answer is **c** 2

6 The answer is **e** 4

7 The answer is **c** 2

8 The answer is **d** 3

9 The answer is **e** 4

10 The answer is **c** 2

11 The answer is **a** 0

12 The answer is **d** 3

13 The answer is **c** 2

14 The answer is **c** 2

15 The answer is **b** 1

16 The answer is **d** 3

17 The answer is **a** 0

18 The answer is **c** 2

19 The answer is **c** 2

20 The answer is **c** 2

Army Test 3

NUMBER DISTANCE

This tests your ability to deal with numbers in your head quickly and accurately. You will need to focus on this task and remember that you are trying to find the number that is the greatest distance from the middle number. The methodical approach is best here. First find the largest and the smallest numbers then work out the distances between these numbers and the remaining number – i.e. from the middle number. (This means the middle number in terms of size rather than the order in which they appear in the sequence – they will often be mixed up in the question rather than being put in the neat order of size.) To get your answer you have to decide which of these numbers – the largest or the smallest – is further away from the number that remains. Remember that the correct answer that you should give will always be either the smallest number or the largest, never the middle number.

Let's look at the first couple of questions to see how this works:

1 The question was 4   3   7

a 4

b 3

c 7

The answer is **c** 7. Here, 7 is the highest number and 3 is the smallest number so we need to concentrate on their relationship to the middle number – 4 – and work out which is furthest away from this middle number. Seven is 3 away from the middle number, whereas the smallest number, 3, is only 1 away. The correct answer must therefore be 7.

2 The question was 9   11   20

a 9

b 11

c 20

The answer is **c** 20. With the middle number being 11, we can see that the lowest number, 9, is 2 away from that. The highest number, 20, is 9 away from 11 so 20, being the furthest away from the middle number must be our answer.

Here is the complete list of answers for this test:

1 The answer is **c** 7

2 The answer is **c** 20

3 The answer is **b** 14

4 The answer is **c** 11

5 The answer is **c** 3

6 The answer is **b** 18

7 The answer is **a** 14

8 The answer is **a** 7

9 The answer is **a** 3

10 The answer is **c** 8

11 The answer is **b** 3

12 The answer is **c** 19

13 The answer is **a** 17

14 The answer is **c** 2

15 The answer is **c** 19

16 The answer is **a** 2

17 The answer is **c** 11

18 The answer is **b** 15

19 The answer is **c** 1

20 The answer is **b** 20

The number distance test will be on your screens in the actual test for just 2 minutes and, as always in the Army tests, the number of questions you get will depend on your speed – so work quickly but accurately.

Army Test 4

ODD ONE OUT

This is essentially a test performed at speed to check your ability to spot the odd one out in a group of words and, of course, to test your understanding of words. You should quickly spot the relationship between two of the words given and the answer will be the word that does not relate to this pair. Each group of three words will contain a pair that is related – they will be either a pair of words that have similar meanings or a pair of words that are opposites. The word that is not part of this pair is, of course, the odd one out.

1 The answer is **b** bus – fat and thin are opposites so bus must be the odd one out.

2   The answer is **a** common – rug and carpet have similar meanings.

3   The answer is **b** also – sail and boat are words that belong together.

4   The answer is **c** drastic – bad and good are opposites.

5   The answer is **a** seven – zoo and animal are words connected to each other but seven is not related to them.

6   The answer is **a** dry – meeting and appointment are similar.

7   The answer is **b** picture – sweet and sour are opposite tastes.

8   The answer is **c** cooperate – dismantle and assemble are opposites.

9   The answer is **a** devious – happy and sad are opposites.

10   The answer is **c** evening – dark and light are opposites.

11   The answer is **a** camera – the words pick and choose are similar.

12   The answer is **c** chair – several and many mean the same.

13   The answer is **a** meet – late and early are opposites.

14   The answer is **b** pullover – sit and stand are opposites.

15   The answer is **a** fall – nasty and nice are opposites.

16   The answer is **c** furniture – coins and change are similar.

17 The answer is **a** sky – a sound and a noise are the same thing.

18 The answer is **a** careful – sleep and doze are two similar actions.

19 The answer is **b** temper – a criminal and a crook are similar.

20 The answer is **c** star – master and mistress are opposites.

Army Test 5

SYMBOL ROTATION

Here you need to be able to turn figures around in your head – and you need to be able to do it quickly. Two different symbols (they are reversed images – or mirror images – of each other) are used in this test so there are only a limited number of rotated figures that can be shown. Below you can see how these two symbols look when they are rotated:

There are two ways that you can ensure a good performance in this test. The first is to imagine that the symbols are anchored by a pin at one edge and then to visualise the figure being rotated. The second way to practise rotating these figures to ensure an improved score is to cut out two symbols from a piece of paper. You will then be able to rotate them and then turn them over (this will make the symbol into its mirror image) so that you can see the combination of figures that can be achieved and understand how the tests work. If you are having problems visualising the symbols rotating, run through the test again using these cutout symbols and it will all become clear.

1 The answer is **b** 1

2 The answer is **c** 2

3 The answer is **a** 0

4 The answer is **c** 2

5 The answer is **b** 1

6 The answer is **c** 2

7 The answer is **b** 1

8 The answer is **a** 0

9 The answer is **b** 1

10 The answer is **c** 2

SECTION 2 – THE NAVY

Navy Test 1

REASONING

In this test you are looking for the connection between the first pair of words so that you can choose a word from the list of answers that has a similar connection to the other word in the question to make a second pair. It tests your verbal reasoning ability and also, of course, the speed at which you can work in this area. Finding the relationship between the two words in the first pair in the question is the key to success here.

1 The answer is **d** week. Here you should have spotted that a minute is part of an hour so you are looking in the answers given for something that is made up of days.

2 The answer is **b** drink. If you are hungry you need food and if you are thirsty you need drink.

3 The answer is **e** initial. If something were last, it would be final in the same way as something first could also be described as initial.

4 The answer is **b** lemon. Sugar tastes sweet so here you are looking for something bitter.

5 The answer is **a** poem. A chapter is part of a book and a verse is part of a poem.

6 The answer is **b** ship. Here you need to find the thing that a rudder is a component of, just as a wheel is part of a car.

7 The answer is **b** day. It is dark at night and light during the day so the answer here should be easy to spot.

8 The answer is **c** starter. A pudding is a dessert so you are looking for a way that soup could be described as part of a meal.

9 The answer is **e** word. A date is a small but important part of a calendar just as a word is part of a book.

10 The answer is **c** few. Several consists of many items and few items could be described as hardly any.

11 The answer is **a** confined. These two phrases are concerned with extent. A limited extent can be expressed as confined, whereas widespread is extensive.

12 The answer is **d** walk. This is a straightforward question asking you to find another word for stroll.

13 The answer is **a** hear. To answer this one correctly you need to know the difference between oral and aural.

14 The answer is **d** library. A coin is a part of money and a book could be a part of a library.

15 The answer is **a** coward. Here you are looking for opposites.

16 The answer is **c** loss. A flaw would destroy perfection so you are looking for an answer to the question 'what would destroy a triumph?'

17 The answer is **a** football. A wicket is where the action is in cricket just as a goalpost is used in the game of football.

18 The answer is **d** defect. The two pairs of words in this questions are synonyms, i.e. have similar meanings.

19 The answer is **b** get hitched. Mate is an informal way to say friend and getting hitched is an informal version of getting married.

20 The answer is **b** pot. An author produces a book and a potter produces a pot.

21 The answer is **a** compact disc. A word is found in a dictionary so you must choose the answer that tells you where a track may be found.

22 The answer is **e** iron. To stitch is what you would do with a sewing machine so you need to find something with which you would press.

23 The answer is **b** radio. You would listen to a radio and view television.

24 The answer is **c** still. The words in this question are two pairs with opposite meanings.

25 The answer is **d** farm. Stock is kept in a warehouse, so where is livestock kept?

26 The answer is **b** oil. Glue would make something sticky so you are looking in the answers for a word that suggests greasiness.

27 The answer is **e** beat. A farmer works in a field so your answer has to be somewhere that a policeman works.

28 The answer is **b** boat. A plane flies and a boat sails.

29 The answer is **c** definition. A clock tells you the time and a dictionary gives you definitions.

30 The answer is **b** train. A car would go along a motorway, just as a train would go along a track.

Navy Test 2

ENGLISH LANGUAGE

The secret to answering these questions is to quickly find something that some of the words have in common. Four of the words listed will be related – they may be adjectives that have similar meanings or they may be various names for similar objects or feelings – and your job is to find that similarity. It will then be easy to spot the one that does not comply.

1 The answer is **c** small. Most of the words in the choice of answers are ones that describe large size whereas only one – small – describes something diminutive, so that is the odd one out.

2 The answer is **e** modest. This is a straightforward opposite meaning to the other four words.

3 The answer is **a** seats. Here the words all describe people who might watch an event. The seats they sit in give you the odd one out.

4 The answer is **d** decisive. Four of the words are anything but decisive.

5 The answer is **b** departure. All the words except departure describe coming back rather than going.

6 The answer is **c** lively. The odd one out is the word that is not a slow, tired condition.

7 The answer is **c** lazy. Four of the words are for conditions that are the opposite of lazy.

8 The answer is **e** order. Another simple opposite to be found.

9 The answer is **d** random. Four of the words suggest a sequence of events but the odd one out – random – suggest no order at all.

10 The answer is **b** inflexible. Four of the words suggest that things can be changed but inflexible does not.

11 The answer is **e** capture. All the words suggest release or freedom with the exception of capture.

12 The answer is **c** respectful. Another opposite for you to find.

13 The answer is **a** gloom. Among all the 'happy' words, gloom stands out as out of place.

14 The answer is **b** just. Tyrannical, despotic, repressive and dictatorial all suggest regimes that are far from just.

15 The answer is **a** decipher. The answer has a sense of order whereas all the others are about disorder.

16 The answer is **e** uncertain. An element of security is to be found in all the words except uncertain.

17 The answer is **d** net. Four of the words describe an amount with no deductions but net is the amount after deductions.

18 The answer is **b** genuine. This is another straightforward case of finding the opposite.

19 The answer is **b** heavy. Four words are lightweight and only one is heavy.

20 The answer is **c** deliberate. All the words describe lack of intent with the exception of deliberate.

21 The answer is **e** balloons. All the words are different celebrations except for balloons – which may be used at the celebration.

22 The answer is **b** narrow. These words describe viewpoint.

23 The answer is **a** indifference. Four of the words concern strong feelings but indifference does not.

24 The answer is **c** depressed. Pleasant feelings make up the rule in this question but the answer suggests unpleasant feelings.

25 The answer is **b** wary. The only word that suggests caution is the answer – wary.

26 The answer is **c** reader. Four of the words are people who write so reader is the odd one out.

27 The answer is **e** adult. All young people except for adult.

28 The answer is **d** destroy. Four of the words involve saving something but destroy means the opposite.

29 The answer is **e** bachelor. Four are female terms so the male term is the odd one out.

30 The answer is **b** factual. Four of the words suggest a lack of truth, so factual is the answer.

Navy Test 3

NUMERACY

1 The answer is **a** 180 miles. Here you must multiply the average speed by the number of hours that the speed was maintained, i.e. $45 \times 4 = 180$. Do not let the mention of 'average speed' put you off.

2 The answer is **d** £2016. This is another multiplication problem. Simply multiply the amount spent per month by the number of months in a year.

3 The answer is **d** 80. If you know that 20% is the same as one-fifth, you can simply divide by 5 to get your answer.

4 The answer is **c** £19.95. The easy way to tackle this is to round the amount up to £4.00, multiply by 5 then deduct the 5×1p.

5 The answer is **e** 30. Simply divide 120 by 4 to get your answer.

6 The answer is **a** £50. Don't let the idea of interest get in the way here, you just need to find 5% of £1000 so divide by 100 and multiply by 5.

7 The answer is **c** 220. Divide by 3 to arrive at one-third.

8 The answer is **b** 40%. Divide 100 (because you are dealing with percentages) by 5 then multiply by 2.

9 The answer is **e** £210. Simply divide by 2 to get one-half.

10 The answer is **b** 82. Divide 123 by 3 to get one-third but don't forget that you are looking for two-thirds – the remaining uniforms – so then multiply by 2.

11 The answer is **b** £9.40. To arrive at 25% you must divide by 4 (or divide by 100 then multiply by 25).

12 The answer is **d** 50%. Five is half – or 50% – of 10.

13 The answer is **b** 12. The easiest way to do this is to divide by 100 to get 1% then multiply by 15 to get your answer.

14 The answer is **c** 48. Here you must multiply 8 by 3, then the answer by 2.

15 The answer is **e** 5.15. This is straightforward – if you are not worried by decimals. Try writing the two figures in a sum on your rough paper, remembering to keep the decimal points aligned.

16 The answer is **b** £11,250. To calculate the discount, divide £12,500 by 10 but do not forget to deduct it from the price to get the amount you will pay after discount.

17 The answer is **d** ⅓. Unless you know this straight away, divide 8 into 24 – as it goes 3 times you know it must be one-third.

18 The answer is **e** ⅒. This relationship between fractions and decimals is important. So long as you realise that 0.1 is the same as ⅒, then you will be able to answer questions like this.

19 The answer is **b** 140. Simply divide by 3 to arrive at one-third.

20 The answer is **a** £1290. Multiplying by 100 is a simple matter of moving the decimal point two places to the right. Of course, some of the answer choices are there to confuse so choose carefully.

21 The answer is **a** £49.50. Divide by 10 to find the amount of the tip but do not forget to add it to the bill to arrive at the total.

22 The answer is **d** £16,100. This is a straightforward subtraction – 20,000 – 2500 – 1400 = 16,100.

23 The answer is **c** 44.5. First work out the overtime worked ((4 × 1) + (0.5)) then add it to the standard working week.

24 The answer is **d** 3 miles. In one hour you would have walked 4 miles so divide by 4 and multiply by 3 to get the distance covered in three-quarters of an hour.

25 The answer is **e** £7.35. This is a straightforward subtraction.

26 The answer is **c** £547. Work out the cost of the games (4 × £12 = £48) then add it to the cost of the computer.

27 The answer is **b** 5 hours. Here you must divide the mileage by the speed to see how long it would take.

28 The answer is **a** $\frac{9}{10}$. Back to fractions. If 0.1 is the same as $\frac{1}{10}$, then 0.9 will be $\frac{9}{10}$.

29 The answer is **b** 25%. As 16 is a quarter of 64, then that is the same as 25%.

30 The answer is **c** 15 minutes. Thirty seconds is half a minute so you would answer 2 questions in a minute – 30 questions would take 15 minutes.

Navy Test 4

MECHANICAL COMPREHENSION

This tests your ability to work with mechanical concepts so an interest in this sort of subject is an obvious help here. You will need to understand how simple machines work, what tools to use for particular jobs and how engineering drawings are made and interpreted. A basic knowledge of mechanical principles will get you through this test.

The majority of the questions in this test are a matter of basic knowledge and there is little point in giving explanations – if you have the knowledge in this area you will choose the correct answer. If, however, you have difficulty with mechanical concepts, read one or two books on the subject. Try to find ones that will give you the basics about how machines work, how gases, solids and liquids react in different situations plus the principles involved in pulleys, levers and motion.

Two general pieces of advice about this sort of test. Firstly, read the questions carefully. Do not, for example, answer a question about controlling temperature as though you have been asked about increasing temperature. Secondly, unless you have absolutely no idea of the correct answer, do not be tempted to guess to save time. There is little point in completing the test but only getting a small number of correct answers because you guessed haphazardly when a little thought and time would have got you a much better result. Where appropriate, a short explanation to questions has been included below.

1   The answer is **a** a drill

2   The answer is **d** gears

3   The answer is **e** a suspension bridge

4   The answer is **a** a blast furnace

5   The answer is **c** a derrick

6   The answer is **b** wood and paper. This question is asking you for knowledge of different fire extinguishers.

7   The answer is **b** a thermostat

8   The answer is **c** an anti-siphon device. This is one that you could work out even if you didn't know the answer. If you know that another word for sucking water is siphoning, then you will know that to stop water being sucked back you would use an anti-siphon device.

9   The answer is **e** a drop in pressure

10 The answer is **e** none of these. A kilo of anything weighs a kilo, no matter how light an individual item may be.

11 The answer is **c** Newton

12 The answer is **a** a barometer

13 The answer is **d** at right angles

14 The answer is **c** a spanner

15 The answer is **a** a low centre of gravity. To answer this question, think about how different sorts of vehicle are stable – or not. A tall or lightweight/vehicle, for example, would be less stable than a low, heavy vehicle.

16 The answer is **b** deceleration

17 The answer is **e** a stopwatch

18 The answer is **c** oxygen

19 The answer is **a** joule

20 The answer is **e** a mitre box. You may use one or two of the other answers when constructing a corner but read the question again – it asks what would MOST help you.

21 The answer is **b** a lever

22 The answer is **a** the sun

23 The answer is **d** 4

24 The answer is **c** mercury

25 The answer is **e** copper. From the answers given, only copper is a good conductor of heat. The others are poor conductors.

26 The answer is **d** 2

27 The answer is **b** magnetic field

28 The answer is **d** a transformer

29 The answer is **c** 1000

30 The answer is **b** tension

SECTION 3 – THE AIR FORCE

Air Force Test 1

VERBAL REASONING

This tests your ability to use written information to answer questions. You will need to understand and interpret what you are being told in the initial information then use that information to reason out the answers to the question. Read the answers and explanations below to see how this works.

1   The answer is **b** Car B. There is only one car that we know has a tow bar and as it is also big enough to accommodate the family of five and is blue, not red, that is the correct car.

2   The answer is **a** Car A. Choose the only hatchback car.

3   The answer is **e** Car E. There are two saloon cars but one of them has a tow bar so choose the one without.

4   The answer is **a** Car A. With no extra seating required but the need to load a wheelchair, the hatchback is the best option.

5   The answer is **c** Car C. There is only one car on offer with metallic paint.

6   The answer is **c** The musical. Bill enjoys musicals.

7   The answer is **e** The Shakespearian comedy. Sita prefers Shakespeare but, of the two on offer, one does not have a matinee performance.

8   The answer is **d** The drama. Declan likes serious drama.

9   The answer is **a** The Shakespearian tragedy. Sita likes Shakespeare and this one has only an evening performance.

10 The answer is **d** The drama. The only choice that is a drama (for Declan) and has a matinee performance (for Sita) is the gritty drama.

The answers to the next five questions can be found by reading – and understanding – the information contained in a paragraph. The questions are straightforward and you are simply being tested here on your ability to locate information in a written piece.

11 The answer is **b** John

12 The answer is **e** Fred

13 The answer is **a** Nelson

14 The answer is **c** Niamh

15 The answer is **d** Steve

The information that will give you the answers to the last five questions in this test is contained in a table so you must become familiar with this format so that you can quickly, easily and accurately deal with information.

16 The answer is **b** Karen and David

17 The answer is **a** Peter

18 The answer is **e** Peter and Meena

19 The answer is **b** Karen

20 The answer is **b** Accounts

Air Force Test 2

NUMERICAL REASONING PART 1

In this test you must prove your ability to work with numbers in the form of fractions and decimals. Make sure that you take advantage of the rough paper that will be available for you. Use it to improve your accuracy with even simple calculations if you are in any doubt. You will have to hand your rough workings in to the invigilator when the test is finished but it will not be marked or taken into account.

1 The answer is **b** 1.0. This is a simple question to get you started, but the choice of answers given can be confusing so you should work carefully to ensure that you choose the right one.

2 The answer is **e** 13. A simple division but, again, some of the answers are close – so don't guess.

3 The answer is **d** 11.1. Keep the decimal point in the right place with this one and you should be OK.

4 The answer is **b** 14. Subtraction, but not written in the usual way.

5 The answer is **c** 1.2. Twelve lots of 0.1 is easy to work out if you understand decimals so if you have any problems, brush up on the basics of decimal calculations.

6 The answer is **a** $\frac{5}{6}$. To solve this one you must find the common denominator – 6 – then convert the elements of the question into sixths ($\frac{2}{6} + \frac{3}{6}$).

7 The answer is **c** 60. If you understand that there are five lots of 0.2 in 1, then you can multiply that by 12 to get your answer of 60.

8 The answer is **e** 25. Simply work this out as a long division (unless you can 'see' the answer straight away).

9 The answer is **c** 36.8. You may find this easier if you deal with the whole numbers first then subtract the decimal.

10 The answer is **c** 50. Don't let the fraction frighten you, this is a straightforward division.

11 The answer is **d** 36. This is very similar to the previous question but using the decimal equivalent of $\frac{1}{2}$.

12 The answer is **b** 48. You could tackle this in two parts – find $\frac{2}{5}$ of 100 then add it to $\frac{2}{5}$ of 20, or simply divide the whole by 5 and multiply by 2.

Air Force Test 3

NUMERICAL REASONING PART 2

This part of the numerical reasoning test assesses your ability to find information in tables, graphs and charts. If you have a problem with numerical information presented in this way you can use all sorts of sources to give you some extra practice. Try reading the annual reports that companies produce, the financial pages in newspapers or statistical information that is presented in this way in magazines or newspapers.

You should take a methodical approach to finding the information you are asked for and make sure that you fully understand the questions. Read through the answers and explanations here to see how this sort of test works and to help you to understand where you may have gone wrong.

1   The answer is **b** £20,000. The only information you need to note from the first sentence in this question is the year. The calculation is $(145-65) - (115-55) = 80-60 = 20$.

2   The answer is **d** £140,000. Read off the value at the top of the stacked column for 2001.

3   The answer is **c** £40,000. The figures to be used in this question go from 95 to 135. Therefore this represents a profit for this department of £40,000.

4   The answer is **d** 2003. A quick visual check should show you the answer here but a more detailed look at the actual profit figures shown on the chart will confirm your answer if you are in any doubt.

5   The answer is **a** £90,000. Here you are being asked to add the figures relating to Rucksacks together – take note that there are only three years that are relevant to this question.

6   The answer is **c** 115. Here you must add together the quantity of people in both groups who prefer soap operas. The danger is that you will simply add together the two percentages rather than working out the number of people these percentages represent. When you are dealing with percentages, but the questions are asking for actual numbers rather than percentages, it is usually a good idea to work out the numbers for each percentage and jot them down. This will prevent you from answering with a percentage when you are being asked for a quantity.

7 The answer is **e** 90. As 30% of over 35s watch sport and there were 300 over 35s in the survey, the calculation is 300 ÷ 100 × 30 = 90.

8 The answer is **a** 22. Here you need to calculate 5% of 200 (under 35s) and 4% of 300 (over 35s) and add your two answers together.

9 The answer is **c** 12. This is similar to the previous question in that you have to do two percentage calculations but then, rather than adding them together, you must subtract one from the other to find the difference.

10 The answer is **d** 86. Here you are working on two parts of the same pie chart and the calculation is Soap Operas 200 ÷ 100 × 20 = 40 + Sport 200 ÷ 100 × 23 = 46. Then add the two together.

11 The answer is **a** Company A. Here you are looking for the steepest upward line for any company over the years 2001 and 2002.

12 The answer is **d** £315,000. In this question you will need to read from the chart (and jot down) the profit for each of the five companies in 2005 then add them together to get your answer. Be extra careful to note from the chart that the answers are in thousands of pounds (£000s) – some of the answers are not and this is done to confuse.

13 The answer is **c** Company C. Here you must concentrate on the years in the question and decide which company shows the biggest increase in profit by the steepest line upwards between the two years.

14 The answer is **a** £10,000. Your first step here is to decide which company was the one to have a fall in profit. It is then a simple task to read off the amount by which that profit decreased.

15 The answer is **b** £55,000. This question aims to prove that you can use information given in charts like this and is a straightforward task of making sure that you read the information for the right year and for the right companies then do the simple calculation with the figures you have noted.

Air Force Test 4

WORK RATE

This tests the speed with which you are able to carry out routine tasks and the coding questions should be worked through as accurately as possible but with speed being your focus. Understanding the instructions before you start the test is essential for success. You will be given examples so you should work through these carefully.

When you have thoroughly understood the way that this test is done, you will be able to complete it without too much trouble. However, your downfall in this test – if you have one – will be inaccuracy so you should work steadily but carefully at this sort of test. So, rather than give explanations for each of the questions, here is a detailed breakdown of how to find the answer to the first question in this test. If you are having difficulty, work through this carefully and it will become clear how it works.

1 The answer is **c** W♦A.

This is a reminder of the grid:

A	D	W	Q
3	5	2	9
□	●	▽	♦

The original code was given in the question as 293. For each of the three items in this code, there are two alternatives. In this example we can see that these alternatives are as follows:

The alternatives to 2 are W and ▽

The alternatives to 9 are Q and ♦

The alternatives to 3 are A and □

These are the letters and symbols that appear in the same columns as the original code. So these three letters and three symbols are the only ones that can appear in the correct answer. You can immediately discard any suggested answers containing D or ●.

As you will see, the instructions dictate that the answer code must not only come from the same columns as the original code but must also be in the same order.

The choice of answers is:

a   W□∇

b   □◆9

c   W◆A

d   ∇◆Q

e   DW□

Start with finding the substitute for 2 in the code. The answer could be either W or ∇, so three of the answers are possibly right. Then look at the next number in the code. The alternatives for 9 are Q and ◆. This limits your list of possible answers to two – **c** W◆A or **d** ∇◆Q. You will then have to check the alternatives to the third number in the code – 3 – to be sure of the correct answer. As the alternatives to 3 are A and □, you can then see that the answer to select must be **c** W◆A.

If you practise using this systematic method for finding the answer, you will soon become more proficient.

2 The answer is **b** 4∇5

3 The answer is **c** ∇T●

4 The answer is **e** ◆HR

5 The answer is **a** ∇53

6 The answer is **d** ∇8□

7 The answer is **d** ●∇R

8 The answer is **b** ◆∇9

9 The answer is **c** W∇P

10 The answer is **a** □●8

11 The answer is **c** Q♦E

12 The answer is **a** 29●

13 The answer is **e** Y3T

14 The answer is **b** 15□

15 The answer is **d** □AF

16 The answer is **e** 19●

17 The answer is **b** T1♦

18 The answer is **c** 9●□

19 The answer is **a** ●□3

20 The answer is **e** G♦V

Air Force Test 5

SPATIAL REASONING PART 1

The first part of this test assesses how well you can fit shapes together and requires an ability to visualise what the shapes would look like when they are joined together. Remember that you must match up the letters that are marked on the shapes so this is a useful and effective starting point for you. The shapes that are the answers to the first two questions are 'exploded' for you below so that you can see how the three shapes in each question have come together, with the x and y sides matching, to make the new shape.

1 The answer is **c**

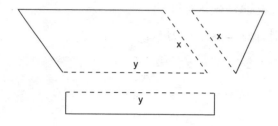

2 The answer is **e**

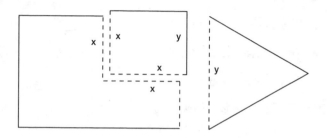

3 The answer is **b**

4 The answer is **a**

5 The answer is **a**

6 The answer is **d**

7 The answer is **e**

8 The answer is **b**

9 The answer is **a**

10 The answer is **d**

Air Force Test 6

SPATIAL REASONING PART 2

The second part of the spatial reasoning test uses three-dimensional objects and requires you to visualise what they will look like when they have been rotated. If you have difficulty with this type of question, note the answers then look back at the objects in the tests so that you can work out how they have been rotated. Pay particular attention to the dots placed on the objects. It may help you if you take note of a particular feature of each drawing – a right angle for example – and then work out where the dot is placed in relation to this.

1 The answer is **d**

2 The answer is **c**

3 The answer is **e**

4 The answer is **d**

5 The answer is **a**

6 The answer is **b**

7 The answer is **d**

8 The answer is **a**

9 The answer is **c**

10 The answer is **e**

Air Force Test 7

ELECTRICAL COMPREHENSION

This test checks your ability to work with electrical concepts. The questions focus on basic principles – such as units of measurement, wiring, resistance, conduction and circuits – and if you are unsure of this information, there are lots of books that will give you the level of knowledge that you need.

Many of the answers to the questions in this part are simple facts (such as the answer to the first question) that you must know if you are to display a knowledge of electrical concepts. If you find that you are having difficulty with this sort of test, then you will need to study a book about basic electrical concepts. Some of the questions, however, require you to understand how those concepts apply so where that is the case, short notes are given to assist you.

1   The answer is **c** resistance

2   The answer is **a** an ammeter

3   The answer is **c** a series circuit

4   The answer is **b** they all go out. For this one, it helps if you know that Christmas tree lights are connected in a series circuit – and we have almost all experienced one bulb failing in those.

5   The answer is **c** parallel circuits

6   The answer is **e** it is the same

7   The answer is **d** amperes

8   The answer is **c** heat, movement and light

9 The answer is **a** a chemical reaction takes place

10 The answer is **d** it would slow down

11 The answer is **b** a variable resistor

12 The answer is **e** ohms

13 The answer is **a** to produce a low voltage direct current

14 The answer is **b** to measure energy provided from a power supply. The second part of the word joulemeter should give you the clue you need that this will measure something.

15 The answer is **d** watts

16 The answer is **a** earth

17 The answer is **e** brown

18 The answer is **b** a fuse

19 The answer is **b** it allows charge to pass safely to earth. The earthing lead prevents sparks that would be created by the static charge.

20 The answer is **a** a thermostat

21 The answer is **d** it needs a large airflow

Air Force Test 8

MECHANICAL COMPREHENSION

Here again you are being tested on your understanding of basic principles and if you are not confident of your abilities in this area, extra preparation will be necessary. Having completed the test in this book, you should have a good idea whether this is a problem area for you. If it is, then get some help in the form of a book on the basic mechanical principles and become familiar with things such as units of measurement, tools, cogs and wheels and simple machinery.

1   The answer is **c** 1000

2   The answer is **b** it is strong

3   The answer is **e** ball bearings

4   The answer is **b** a drawing pin. This requires you to know that a small surface area (such as the point of a pin or the blade of a knife) concentrates pressure whereas a larger surface area (such as a table top or the top of a drawing pin) spreads out the pressure.

5   The answer is **b** brittle

6   The answer is **d** Plimsoll line

7   The answer is **b** Newton's

8   The answer is **b** acceleration

9   The answer is **e** viscosity

10 The answer is **c** chemical energy

11 The answer is **e** friction

12 The answer is **d** mass and velocity

13 The answer is **a** centripetal

14 The answer is **e** it increases

15 The answer is **b** oil

16 The answer is **c** freons

17 The answer is **a** a bimetallic strip

18 The answer is **b** solids

19 The answer is **a** a demodulator

20 The answer is **c** sound. Think of a guitar or violin string to get your answer to this one.

AIR FORCE TEST 9

MEMORY PART 1

Note that both parts of this test – to check your ability to remember information accurately – will be presented to you on film. Obviously, it is not possible to replicate this test in a book but if you carry out the practice tests, you will see exactly what you have to do and whether or not you need to improve your memory.

The first part of this test asks you to recall a sequence of letters and work out how many letters were between the two that you are given in the question. Most people would find they are more successful when they try to visualise the sequence. There is little point to written explanations for this sort of test as you can simply go back to the test and check the actual answer and see where you went wrong. Practice is the best solution if you are having problems with memory tests. Apart from doing more tests of this sort, you could try, during your everyday life, to improve your memory – perhaps by making more effort to remember telephone numbers, shopping lists, PIN numbers and so on. Practice at remembering any type of sequence will help you to improve your performance in this sort of test.

1 The answer is **b** 4

2 The answer is **c** 1

3 The answer is **a** 4

4 The answer is **b** 0

5 The answer is **d** 1

6 The answer is **d** 2

7 The answer is **a** 4

8 The answer is **d** 1

9 The answer is **c** 2

10 The answer is **c** 2

Air Force Test 10

MEMORY PART 2

The second part of the memory test is checking your ability to recall patterns and combine them to make a new pattern. Again, visualising the grids and combining them in your imagination is how you should tackle this task. Don't forget that the grids will be shown to you on film and you will only see one grid at a time so you will have to keep the pattern of each one in your memory until you see the suggested answers.

There are two ways that you can try to improve your performance in this sort of test. You can either try to memorise the individual grids and then find the answer grid that combines them or you can try to combine the grids in your memory, get an overall picture of the answer grid in your mind and then look for that in the suggested answers. You will be able to go back and try out these alternatives on the test given in Chapter 2 as it is unlikely that you will remember the answers from the first time you completed the test – the grids will have been committed only to your short-term memory.

1 The answer is **d**

2 The answer is **b**

3 The answer is **a**

4 The answer is **c**

5 The answer is **b**

6 The answer is **d**

7 The answer is **c**

8 The answer is **a**

9 The answer is **d**

10 The answer is **b**

CHAPTER 5

Diagnosis and further reading

By reading the notes in the explanation chapter and recording the number of questions you have got right and how many you got wrong, you should have been able to assess your aptitude in each area and to see where extra practice and preparation is necessary.

As each of the Armed Forces has different testing criteria, we will now look at them one by one:

THE ARMY

As we saw previously, the test for entry as a soldier is constructed so that there is no 'pass or fail'. Rather it is used as an assessment of your aptitudes and your potential. Some areas of work require a relatively low score in the test while other trades demand high scores plus relevant qualifications to be accepted for training in that area. The higher your overall score, the more options for training you will be offered. By improving your performance you can give yourself a greater choice of trades. The personnel at the recruiting offices are usually extremely helpful and will be willing to discuss the options with you.

The tests are all carried out via a touch screen (although keyboard and computer skills are not necessary to sit the test) and then your results are analysed to show the best fit within the Army for your aptitudes. This analysis, completed by computer, uses a complicated formula that weights your answers in the various areas, takes into account how quickly you worked through each individual part and assesses your potential in a number of areas. Also, the number of questions asked in each part can vary according to the aptitude you show in that particular part. For these reasons it is not possible to accurately evaluate your score in the overall test without the use of the Army's computer program. You can, however, keep a tally of your score in each practice test and use this to check your progress and to see which area you need to give more attention.

THE NAVY

As the tests for the Navy can be assessed as to whether they are right or wrong and everyone is given the same number of questions to answer, it is possible to evaluate your score more accurately.

To check your progress in any of the test areas, go through all of the tests that you have completed and give yourself 5 marks for each correct answer. For each test there is a potential 'raw' score of 150 (5 marks for each of the 30 questions).

Mark each answer as correct or incorrect. Each question correctly answered scores 5 marks as follows.

Correct answers	1	2	3	4	5	6	7	8	9	10
Score	5	10	15	20	25	30	35	40	45	50

Incorrect answers score 0 points.

For example, a test with 26 questions correct, 3 incorrect, 1 not attempted, would score as follows:

26 correct × 5 marks = 130
3 incorrect × 0 marks = 0
1 incomplete × 0 = 0

Test score = 130

Now use the following charts to interpret your final score for each test:

Well below average	Below average	Above average	Well above average
0 to 45	50 to 80	85 to 125	130 or over

If your score is 'Above average' or 'Well above average', you may decide that you would like to spend more of your preparation time on other parts of the test. If the results indicate that your score is 'Below average' or 'Well below average', keep practising. Go through the test again in that area and read the explanations carefully. As you work through the tests, you should see an improvement in the scores you achieve.

Whatever your score, do not allow yourself to be discouraged – tests are only part of the interview process and it is possible to improve with practice.

THE AIR FORCE

In the Air Force tests, as with those for the Navy, you can record your answers. Work out a score for each test (by allocating 5 points for each correct answer as above) and then use the following charts to evaluate your scores according to the particular test:

Verbal Reasoning, Work Rate, Spatial Reasoning and Mechanical Comprehension

Maximum raw score 100

NB Add your scores from the two parts of the spatial reasoning test together.

Well below average	Below average	Above average	Well above average
0 to 25	30 to 50	55 to 80	85 or over

Numerical Reasoning

Maximum raw score 135

NB Add your scores from the two parts of this test together.

Well below average	Below average	Above average	Well above average
0 to 45	50 to 75	80 to 115	120 or over

Electrical Comprehension

Maximum raw score 105

Well below average	Below average	Above average	Well above average
0 to 30	35 to 55	60 to 85	90 or over

SUGGESTIONS FOR FURTHER IMPROVEMENT

Problems and pitfalls

Now that you have worked through the questions, answers and explanations, we can look at the problems and pitfalls associated with tests in general. For example, it is absolutely essential that you read the instructions carefully. Ask yourself a few questions as you read:

- What exactly are you being asked to do?

- How should you indicate your answers?

- Can you write on the question paper?

- Has some spare paper been supplied for the purpose of rough calculations or for jotting down notes?

- Do you need to estimate the answer?

These are general things that you should look out for but there are also some pitfalls that are associated with specific types of questions. You will find many of these highlighted in this book when the individual questions are explained – see Chapter 4. Here are a few guidelines for avoiding some of the problems and pitfalls you may come across:

- With tests where you have to write your answers on a separate sheet of paper, check from time to time that you are writing your answers in the right place. It is easy – especially if you have to miss out a difficult question or are working under time constraints – to continue down the answer sheet totally unaware that your answers are wrong simply because they are written in the wrong space.

- Avoid spending too much time on a difficult question.

- Don't guess. You may need to estimate an answer in the numerical parts or make a reasoned selection in the other tests but do not resort to wild guessing.

The value of preparation

Unfamiliarity gets in the way of your natural ability, so practice is an invaluable form of preparation. An Olympic runner does not just turn up at the track and set off as fast as he can – he will practise extensively, treat his mind and body well and find out all he can about the race. Why should taking any other sort of test be different? So make the most of your period of preparation. Practice is the most important element of your preparation strategy. The timed tests in Chapter 2 will help with that. Aim to practise for up to 2 hours in any one session. Any more than that may be counter-productive. It is almost impossible to sustain the intense concentration needed for any longer than 2 hours.

What other forms of preparation should you consider? Apart from the intensive practice that you can take advantage of by using the tests in this book, there are other sorts of practice. For example, to help with the numerical tests you should make yourself aware of the numbers that are all around you – and use them as opportunities for practice.

- When you are shopping in the supermarket, estimate what your total bill will be or continually calculate how much you can save by buying one product rather than another, or the cost of a single item contained in a multi-pack, or the cost per 100 ml or 100 g based on a larger packet or container.

- Notice the data that is presented to you every day in the financial pages of newspapers. This will involve increases, decreases and percentages.

● Seek out numerical information in company reports or in trade magazines.

● Use train timetables to gain familiarity with using information presented in this way.

● Practise using currency exchange rates given in newspapers or by your travel agent.

● Brush up on using fractions, square roots, multiplication tables, percentages and decimals.

● If you usually use a calculator, put it away and practise without it. You will not be allowed to use one during the assessment.

The test itself

Tests will be timed and not much time will be allowed for you to do the tests – it will be tight – and it is frequently not possible to complete all the tests in the time allotted. Do not let this worry you.

Even when you are sitting in the test room, you can still improve your chances of success. There are a few important things to remember at this stage:

● Listen to – and be sure to comply with – the instructions given by the test administrator.

● Read the instructions on the test paper – these may cover items such as:

○ How much time you will be allowed

○ Whether or not you may write on the margins of the test paper or if rough paper is supplied for your workings

○ How you should indicate your answer – with a tick or a cross for example

○ What to do if you want to change one of your answers.

If you don't understand something at this stage – before the test begins – speak up. There are sometimes example questions that you will be instructed to read before the timed test begins. Use the time allowed for this to ensure that you understand exactly what you are being asked to do. Don't try to pretend that you know everything – you do not need to impress the other candidates.

Read the questions carefully. Although you will be trying to work quickly, there is no point in answering all the questions but getting many of them wrong because you did not understand what was required.

Go through the questions methodically – don't be tempted to rush on to later questions first. Some papers may be structured so that the questions get progressively more difficult – if you look at the later questions first, you may not make the best use of your time.

Strategy

The main strategy during the test will involve timing – see below – but you may also want to consider how much you will use your powers of estimation. Here again, practice will help. Some questions on a numerical reasoning test are ideal for estimation. Rounding up or down can often be a quick way of arriving at the only possible answer from those given in multiple-choice questions.

If you are really struggling with a particular question, do not waste time. Finding a difficult question can be unnerving. Far better to move on — there may be later questions that you find easy.

Try not to let people around you affect your performance. Just because the person at the next desk has turned over a lot more pages than you, it does not mean that you are doing badly. They might have all their answers wrong!

Timing

The time allowed for the various tests that you will undertake will vary according to the type of test.

The important thing is to use your time wisely. It is rare that too much time will be allowed for a test. It is far more likely that you will run out of time. You will therefore need to work quickly while trying to be as accurate as possible. Try not to let one question take up too much of your time. If a particular question is proving difficult for you, move on. You can always come back to it if you find that you have plenty of time.

ON THE DAY

You must plan to arrive at the test centre in a state that is conducive to achieving your best possible score. This means being calm and focused. It is possible that you may feel nervous before the test, but you can help yourself by preparing in advance the practical details that will enable you to do well. Remember, it is unlikely that you are the only person who is feeling nervous; what is important is how you deal with your nerves! The following suggestions may help you to overcome unnecessary test-related anxiety.

1 Know where the test centre is located, and estimate how long it will take you to get there – plan your 'setting off time'. Now plan to leave 45 minutes before your setting off time to allow for travel delays. This way, you can be more or less certain that you will arrive at the test centre in good time. If, for any reason, you think you will miss the start of the session, call the administrator to ask for instructions.

2 Try to get a good night's sleep before the test. This is obvious advice and, realistically, it is not always possible, particularly if you are prone to nerves the night before a test. However, you can take some positive steps to help. Consider taking a hot bath before you go to bed, drinking herbal rather than caffeinated tea, and doing some exercise. Think back to what worked last time you took an exam and try to replicate the scenario.

3 The night before the test, organise everything that you need to take with you. This includes test instructions, directions, your identification, pens, erasers, possibly your calculator (with new batteries in it), reading glasses, and contact lenses.

4 Decide what you are going to wear and have your clothes ready the night before. Be prepared for the test centre to be unusually hot or cold, and dress in layers so that you can regulate the climate yourself. If your test will be preceded or followed by an interview, make sure you dress accordingly for the interview which is likely to be a more formal event than the test itself.

5 Eat breakfast! Even if you usually skip breakfast, you should consider that insufficient sugar levels affect your concentration and that a healthy breakfast might help you to concentrate, especially towards the end of the test when you are likely to be tired.

6 If you know that you have specific or exceptional requirements which will require preparation on the day, be sure to inform the test administrators in advance so that they can assist you as necessary. Similarly, if you are feeling unusually unwell on the day of the test, make sure that the test administrator is aware of it.

7 If, when you read the test instructions, there is something you don't understand, ask for clarification from the administrator. The time given to you to read the instructions may or may not be limited but, within the allowed time, you can usually ask questions. Don't assume that you have understood the instructions if, at first glance, they appear to be similar to the instructions for the practice tests.

8 Don't read through all the questions before you start. This simply wastes time. Start with Question 1 and work swiftly and methodically through each question in order. Unless you are taking a computerised test where the level of difficulty of the next question depends on you correctly answering the previous question, don't waste time on questions that you know require a lot of time. You can return to these questions at the end if you have time left over.

9 After you have taken the test, find out the mechanism for feedback, and approximately the number of days you will have to wait to find out your results. Ask whether there is scope for objective feedback on your performance for your future reference.

10 Celebrate that you have finished.

FURTHER SOURCES OF PRACTICE

In this final part you will find a list of useful sources for all types of psychometric tests.

Books

Barrett, J., *Test Yourself! Test Your Aptitude, Personality and Motivation, and Plan Your Career*. London: Kogan Page, 2000.

Bolles, Richard N., *The 1997 What Colour Is Your Parachute?* Berkeley, CA: Ten Speed Press, 1997.

Carter, P. and K. Russell, *Psychometric Testing: 1000 Ways to Assess Your Personality, Creativity, Intelligence and Lateral Thinking*. Chichester: John Wiley, 2001.

Chin-Lee, Cynthia, *It's Who You Know*. Toronto, ON: Pfeiffer, 1993.

Cohen, D., *How to Succeed at Psychometric Tests*. London: Sheldon Press, 1999.

Crozier, G., *Test Your Verbal Reasoning*. London: Hodder & Stoughton, 2000.

Jackson, Tom, *The Perfect Résumé*. New York: Doubleday, 1990.

Kourdi, Jeremy, *Succeed at Psychometric Testing: Practice Tests for Verbal Reasoning (Advanced Level)*. London: Hodder & Stoughton, 2004.

Nuga, Simbo, *Succeed at Psychometric Testing: Practice Tests for Verbal Reasoning (Intermediate Level)*. London: Hodder & Stoughton, 2004.

Parkinson, M., *How to Master Psychometric Tests*. London: Kogan Page, 1997.

Pelshenke, P., *How to Win at Aptitude Tests*. Kettering: Thorsons, 1993.

Rhodes, Peter S., *Succeed at Psychometric Testing: Practice Tests for Diagrammatic and Abstract Reasoning*. London: Hodder & Stoughton, 2004.

Smith, Heidi, *How to Pass Numerical Reasoning Tests: A Step-by-Step Guide to Learning the Basic Skills*. London: Kogan Page, 2002.

Tolley, H. and K. Thomas, *How to Pass Verbal Reasoning Tests*. London: Kogan Page, 2001.

Vanson, Sally, *Succeed at Psychometric Testing: Practice Tests for Data Interpretation*. London: Hodder & Stoughton, 2004.

Walmsley, Bernice, *Succeed at Psychometric Testing: Practice Tests for Numerical Reasoning (Intermediate Level)*. London: Hodder & Stoughton, 2004.

Walmsley, Bernice, *Succeed at Psychometric Testing: Practice Tests for Numerical Reasoning (Advanced Level)*. London: Hodder & Stoughton, 2004.

Walmsley, Bernice, *Succeed at Psychometric Testing: Practice Tests for The National Police Selection Process*. London: Hodder & Stoughton, 2005.

Test publishers and suppliers

Assessment for Selection and Employment
Chiswick Centre
414 Chiswick High Road
London W4 5TF
telephone: 0208 996 3337

Oxford Psychologists Press
Elsfield Hall
15–17 Elsfield Way
Oxford OX2 8EP
telephone: 01865 404500

Saville & Holdsworth Ltd
The Pavilion
1 Atwell Place
Thames Ditton
Surrey KT7 0SR
telephone: 0208 398 4170

The Psychological Corporation
32 Jamestown Road
London NW1 7BY

The Test Agency Ltd
Burgner House
4630 Kingsgate
Oxford Business Park South
Oxford OX4 2SU
telephone: 01865 402900

Useful websites

Websites are prone to change, but the following are correct at
the time of going to press.

www.army.mod.uk/careers

www.armyjobs.co.uk

www.ase-solutions.co.uk

www.bhgplc.com

www.bps

www.careerpsychologycentre.com

www.careers-uk.com

www.cipd.org.uk

www.deloitte.co.uk/index.asp

www.englishforum

www.englishtogo

www.ets.org

www.freesat1prep.com

www.guardian.co.uk/money

www.home.g2a.net

www.kogan-page.co.uk

www.mensa.org.uk

www.mod.uk/careers

www.morrisby.co.uk

www.newmonday.co.uk

www.oneclickhr.com

www.opp.co.uk

www.pgcareers.com/apply/how/recruitment.asp

www.psychtesting.org.uk

www.pwcglobal.com/uk/eng/carinexp/undergrad/quiz.html

www.publicjobs.gov.ie/numericatest.asp

www.puzz.com

www.rafcareers.com

www.rinkworks.com/brainfood.maths.html

www.royal-navy.mod.uk

→ The Armed Forces (Entry Level)

www.testagency.co.uk

www.tests-direct.com

www.thewizardofodds.xom/math/group1.html

Useful organisations

American Psychological Association Testing and Assessment

Association of Recognised English Language Schools (ARELS)

Australian Psychological Society

The Best Practice Club

The British Psychological Society

Canadian Psychological Society

The Chartered Institute of Marketing

The Institute of Personnel and Development

Psyconsult

Singapore Psychological Society

Society for Industrial and Organisational Assessment (South Africa) (SIOPSA)